D1614174

DISCLAIMER

Some of the language contained in the book "The Endless Beginning" may be offensive to some readers. The opinions of characters in this book do not necessarily reflect opinions of the author or the publisher. The book has to be read in its entirety to discern the underlying messages in it. Any resemblance of characters, past or present, to actual individuals is completely coincidental with exception of well-known historical figures.

Table of Contents

Chapter 1

A journey into the Abyss

August 21,1969

In the law office of Emil Chaikin JD, the day began inconspicuously; few legal briefs to be filed, a short trip to the courthouse, and then the usual paperwork related to current cases. One of the envelopes that caught his attention immediately was a letter from the Passport Authority notifying Mother Mary that a temporary visa to Romania and Yugoslavia was granted with a return date of August 29, 1969. The application was of course intended to trick the KGB into issuing passports to the Chaikin family, a family on a KGB watch list of people not allowed out of the country at any cost.

Attorney Chaikin was in hot water again. In 1967, after the victorious six days war with Soviet-supported Egypt, the KGB caught on that letters from Israel were being sent regularly to Emil's office.

He was summoned to the local branch, forced to wait four hours in front of State Security legal counsel's office, and when finally invited in 15 minutes before 5 PM, told, "We know everything. You are not only an American spy, but a Zionist snake also."

This was an absurd and idiotic statement even by KGB standards since there were years of evidence starting in 1941 that Emil had been a legal

guardian of hundreds of Jewish children and
families subsequently sent to Palestine and later to
Israel. He was the only link to families they never
knew and would send him a letter just to talk to
someone they trusted.

"My children," he would say, opening the
latest letter from Israel.

The Arab defeat changed all that, and now
the Jewish State was the new enemy on the block.
Anyone in touch with Israel was on a watch list.

"Only the historic changes instituted by our
beloved leader, First Secretary of CPSU Comrade
Khrushchev, prevent us from sending you and your
treacherous family back to a labor camp," the
Legal Counsel noted.

The threat was so high that a message was
sent through a secret channel to Haifa asking the
children to stop writing letters immediately.

This was not Emil's only trouble. He was
well known as a staunch anti-communist leader of
the resistance against the Red Terror, a terror that
had claimed the life of his brother-in-law Rangel
and sent his sister Elsa to the terror camp of
Belene.

So it was no surprise when a respected
Bulgarian mathematician named Mrs. Baker
walked into his office with a secret: she was dying
from breast cancer, had been left in deep cover by
American OSS in 1942, and wanted him to be the
legal guardian of her estate and two daughters
because she suspected her husband was a KGB
informant who might hurt the children.

Ordinarily, she would have been thrown out
of his office as an obvious KGB plant. Someone
pretending to be a foreign agent was a textbook
joke, and all undercover infiltrators wore state-

issued brown shoes, available only to the KGB.

But this time, the fate rolled a real die. Emil had known her and the family for years and knew for certain that her husband was an informant, having obtained via an underground source a copy of his reports to the KGB.

He arranged for her to be sent to the Vatican Hospital for treatment, which proved futile, as the cancer had already spread and she had been given less than three months to live. It was unknown who paid for the trip or if she got in touch with her handlers, but immediately after her return, KGB agents swarmed in her apartment, confiscating every piece of paper without court orders. It was their habit to kick the front door first and announce themselves later.

Mrs. Baker died in late July, followed by an immediate legal confrontation with her husband. Encouraged by the KGB, he made a claim of property and parental rights over the children.

Fortunately, Emil had full power of attorney, and even in a country where law was arbitrary and often ignored, the opposition had to retreat, though not for long. From underground reports it became plain that the husband was getting dirty by the day, having claimed that Mrs. Baker was in fact an American agent and hence must have left a secret list of agents and codes in the custody of her attorney.

This made it necessary for Emil to be out of the country by August 29th, 1969 or face a prolonged and painful spy investigation, which, even without any merit, in the hands of lunatics like KGB could turn into a dangerous spiral with no way out.

In addition, Emil's oldest son Alex had received a summons from the military district to

report for six months of training as a tank
commander. He was to be posted on the Soviet Far
Eastern border at Usury River when tensions
between the two Communist superpowers had
flared in bloody confrontations where hundreds of
soldiers were mutilated in a display of barbarity not
seen since World War II.

The only way to be excused or be granted a
delay from the assignment was to get a University
letter of enrollment in the fall semester of 1969, a
favor that a friend in the underground was happy to
provide.

At the same time, the Secret Services had
begun to use mind drugs on prisoners instead of
their proven medieval tortures. According to recent
accounts, some people were let out of custody
unable to recognize their family members and left
without any mental associations, walking around
town like zombies. Thus the Communists had
changed the old motto from "If you are not with us,
you are against us," to, "If you are not with us, we
will make you a living dead."

In this environment, the family had to plan
and act swiftly, driving out of town every day to
avoid KGB eavesdropping and detection, going so
far as to remove all books and handwritten notes
that could indicate intent or associations.

The old Trabant was traded for a converted
WWII ambulance on August 23rd, 1969 so the car
could use a temporary license plate, depriving the
police of the time to make the connection of who
was traveling in it and why.

On advice of a trusted friend Dr. Randolph
Rogalsky, a world authority on ancient numismatic
coins, a stealthy acquisition of silver Roman
sestertius and Greek drachmas was initiated as

7

difficult days loomed ahead.

August 24th, 1969 was a breezy, bright day with an ink-blue sky as the family left ancient town of Varna on the Black Sea toward the nearest Romanian border crossing at the Danube River, following a row of cars on the winding road north.

Everything was going well for about 30 minutes when Alex, glancing at the side-view mirror, noticed a yellow scooter with two men suddenly passing the car behind and then staying right on his bumper. A second look brought even more fear: the driver was a known KGB informant.

It has been said by old people that when man gets depressed, even his horse won't run. Sure enough, the temperature indicator of the old ambulance was creeping up until the unmistakable smell of boiling antifreeze meant only one thing: pull over or else.

The two goons in the back also pulled over, an indication that the KGB was playing the usual cat-and-mouse game of vicious curiosity with their victims, a game usually preceding an arrest followed by the feared interrogation.

But for the time being, Alex had only to worry about fixing the overheating engine or risk return to town in the open arms of the Secret Police.

A quick look at engine compartment made it clear that the culprit was the old thermostat, held in place by two rusted bolts, one of which was so stripped that a cut across had to be filed in order to remove the offending part.

Back on the road again, the two goons on the yellow scooter passed them at high speed and vanished in fields ahead, probably to warn a KGB detail on the next intersection to pull them over.

It's difficult for a loving family to wait for forty-some excruciating minutes to find out if the Providence will intervene and let them be free or be torn apart and spend years of torture and degradation in jail. Their teary eyes and heavy hearts pulsed every second to the faithful resolution of this real drama.

In cases like this, there is only one thing a person can do. Mother Mary offered a prayer that the man called Immanuel, with a shadow and hands of living gold, would make himself visible and lead them away from the evil of the KGB, away forever in the land of the free and home of the brave, America.

Someone must have heard the prayer. By the time they were at the border crossing, there was no sign of the goons with the yellow scooter or a KGB detail, just a line of twenty cars waiting to be processed by the border police.

Alex decided to use a psychological trick, hoping to avoid a police search since all numismatic coins were tucked under the seats floor beam, and the chance of finding them was high. For each coin, they could get at least two years in prison, and they had fifty in all.

The old ambulance was parked and raised on a jack stand with the brothers pretending to be working underneath.

The Chief of the Border Police could not believe the audacity of these obnoxious people fixing an old junk car right in front of his office. In his fury, he gave the brothers sixty-seconds to get the car out and in the fast line border section. The passports were flashed, and the family was literally thrown out without any search at all.

The first step had been widely successful,

and then there was a long drive through mountain's back roads designed to avoid an encounter with KGB search teams as the family drove toward Yugoslavian border. In Belgrade, they got a bit of good news; for a bottle of fine Bulgarian cognac, a Serbian policeman divulged the name of a border station near the Austrian City of Graz where security was not as tight or precise as other points along the frontier. As the old ambulance rolled along winding roads of the mountains and the night blanketed everything with sticky, impenetrable darkness amplified by an occasional blast of rain showers and patches of fog, it was time for Father Emo to take the wheel since Alex had driven for almost eleven hours, bordering on collapse from physical exhaustion.

An hour must have passed when everyone was awakened by a loud noise and the sound of screeching brakes: Father Emo had fallen asleep at the wheel and the car hit and penetrated a safety wall with the left front wheel protruding over a 100-foot cliff. It took some time to pull out of the mangled steel embankment, but the last two hours were in the hands of Alex, the most experienced driver to lead them on the way to the border.

The family was advised by the Bulgarian underground to park the car at least a half mile away, possibly behind a small hill, then crawl to the border fence and use the two foot-long wooden planks to make an opening for an entry, and never, ever cut the wire. It was well known that this would almost certainly trigger a position sensor, guiding the guards right to them.

Two hours passed in a flash of tense expectation as the family soon was able to see the border crossing to the left as Alex went off the road

10

and hid the old ambulance in a hollow covered by young pine trees and small brush.

He carefully crossed the road and crawled to the top of the hill and then his heart missed a beat. There it was, the long, barbed-wire fence, meandering away from the checkpoint, surrounded by meadows on the Serbian side and a tall alpine forest on the other side. It seemed that there was no one around, so he just ran along the meadow to the wire and then hit the ground. Now was time to pull the two lowest wires apart with the wood planks and carefully slide under on the other side. Fortunately, there was no electricity in the wire, and soon he was facing a field of about forty feet of freshly raked ground as best he could see in darkness interrupted by occasional flashes of starlight as ragged clouds flew above.

The raked ground meant that if there was a minefield across the fence, it had to be electrically operated; otherwise, contact mines would have blown the tractor operator to pieces.

Alex was advised to put about twenty large, flat pebbles in his pocket, face the field, choose a direction of below or above 45 degrees to his face with his right hand, then throw a pebble and wait for a reaction. If it hit a land mine, the exercise was over, and he would be on the right side of the Lord for sure; otherwise, throw another pebble at some two feet in the same good direction and keep carefully stepping over the iridescent markers until he hopefully made it across the field.

Soon he was on the other side of the raked ground, facing an enormous pine forest and seeing through the brush the Austrian checkpoint some 500 feet away.

A pair of bright eyes flew out of the forest,

and Alex was knocked to the ground by a big guard dog, growling, teeth right on his neck, warning not to move or else.

That fear was on Alex's mind is an understatement, yet because of his past experience in training dogs, he felt that he was placed under arrest and not attacked, so unless he moved his arms, everything would be all right. After all, this was obviously a trained Austrian police dog with a rank of at least a sergeant.

"Good girl, very good girl," he started whispering when he felt that the dog was actually very gentle with her hind legs and teeth around his neck.

"I love you girl, my beautiful girl."

Alex had small candies in his left pocket and offered her some, knowing very well that the first thing a police dog is taught is not to accept food from anyone but the handler. But she could not resist the treat, and after licking his face with her long rough tongue, let him sit up with his legs folded. In other words, he was under arrest, but under friendlier terms than before.

When the Austrian guard finally arrived, he could not believe his eyes; his darling dog was sitting next to a very suspicious person in the middle of the night, and worst of all, the stranger had his left hand around her neck, gently scratching her behind the ears.

"Halt, what are you doing here? What is your name?"

Alex stated he is requesting a political asylum and his family was on the other side waiting for directions.

"Go back and bring them in," the man said.

"We will discuss the matter later."

Full of joy that all so far has gone well and forgetting about the raked ground for a moment, Alex started walking back, not even following his own footsteps until he saw the sign "Mines" right on the other side of the fence facing Austria. It has been reported by wise people that at a critical juncture, your whole life flashes before you. As he stood on his left leg, the right one about two feet from the nearest pebble, trying not to lose balance and come crashing down on the soft ground below, Alex saw all that wonderful life, every bit of it as if a photographic tape played in a millionth of a second. Carefully stepping down on the pebble and retracing his own steps backwards, he was back on the other side of the fence and then fell down on the ground and burst into tears. If some great hero ever told you that men don't cry even when facing death, he was probably lying since the only way someone realizes how much their life means is when he or she is about to lose it.

After brushing the tears away, he walked back to his family and led them toward the top of the hill and to the fence. The family had to hit the ground fast since there were four or five Serbian soldiers walking by the fence, illuminating the ground with searchlights, a clear indication that Alex must have tripped a buried sensor somewhere.

They went back to the old car and without pushing the gas too much, carefully approached the checkpoint to see no one in sight and the bar left unlocked. Alex lifted it up, and they rushed across to the Austrian side.

The Austrian guards would not let them in unless they requested political asylum, but after a short standoff, the family was let through with directions to drive to the Vienna suburb of Treis Kirchen for processing.

At about 2 AM, exhausted from the unbearable stress of the crossing, Alex had to pull off the winding road and look for a safe place to spend the rest of the night before resuming the trip to the capital city. On the right side, he found a hidden, flat brushy meadow next to a nearly vertical cliff and a patch of alpine forest below, a perfect place to be away from the preying eyes of the road. It was well known that the KGB had the bad habit of sending execution teams after their enemies.

Two tents were huddled under the pines, and for first time in twenty-eight hours, the family fell asleep without worry about tomorrow. Alex was left to stand guard through the rest of the night, holding in hand the only weapon they had, a WWII dagger the border patrol had failed to confiscate.

Sudden gusts of wind made the rocks up the cliff cry in a strange dissonant harmony and tall pines groaned and moaned as patches of white-gray clouds ran across the sky, with Alex holding the knife in his sweat-soaked hand.

Then the wind stopped, and silence covered the meadow as his lead-heavy eyelids started closing in a sleepy dream, when suddenly Alex heard a noise of someone walking slowly toward him from the pine forest.

"My God, they found us, somehow they found us even here," he thought as he stood up to face the threat.

"Who is there?" The noise of the footsteps stopped.

"Hey, where are you?" he said as he pointed the flashlight toward the winding trail

14

vanishing in the dark bowels of heavy brush.

"Maybe an animal on the loose," he thought, his heart still beating fast as he sat down with his back against a tree. His eyes still tired and closing fast, Alex must have snoozed for a bit when he heard the footsteps again. This time he lost it all and simply wanted to kill this thing or die and get it over with. Dagger in one hand, light in the other, he ran toward the forest, screaming, "Come here and face me, you son of a bitch, or I will find you and cut you to pieces!"

The sound of footsteps seem to run back and fade in the forest as Alex stopped, heart beating madly, eyes full of tears, blood dripping from his hand as he had cut himself in the hurdle.

"I have to sleep now, and if I don't wake up tomorrow, let it be."

He drove the dagger into the soft ground, bandaged his bleeding hand, and lay down on the side of the tent, covering himself with young pine branches.

Alex woke up with the sun flashing behind the tall trees and the sweet smell of homemade soup coming from the fire over which Mother Mary had suspended her small pot. At the same time, she was baking potatoes, and whole eggs were buried in the hot ashes of large chunks of pine bark she had collected from the forest.

Alex was hungry, very hungry, but the eerie encounter was still on his mind, so clutching the dagger in his left hand, he cautiously started walking toward the forest trail where the footsteps had vanished in the dark of the night. There was nothing out of the ordinary, just a lot of brush surrounding a small clearing in the midst of a pine forest directly from the fairy tales of Brothers

Grimm. He heard noise on the side of the cliff of someone breaking small twigs, and when he looked, there it was; an enormous Saint Bernard dog, small bag on the neck collar, digging the forest soil with its paw, looking at him with its big, reddish eyes.

Great conquerors of the past have learned from bitter experience that before you attack someone, it is helpful to have a plan for retreat in case things don't pan out as expected, but he never had such an encounter, just anger and frustration after many hours of stress and danger.

He grabbed a good-size pine trunk from the ground, cleaned it up with the dagger, and ran after the dog straight toward the cliff, screaming in rage:

"You son of a bitch, you gave me a heart attack last night and I will whip your Saint Bernard ass right now!"

But soon the dog was at the end of the trail, facing the cliff with no place to go but back. It turned around, looking at him with the eyes of an angry schoolteacher, and Alex then realized he was in trouble, with an injured right hand and the dagger in the left hand, facing a 150-pound Saint Bernard canine with teeth of a monster.

So the wood stick flew away as he was running for dear life, with the warm breath of the dog right at his back and enjoying the chase, having licked his neck a couple of times.

Alex dove in one of the tents, and then the dog made its tactical mistake, body flying at the speed of sound and unable to turn fast, it collided with Mother Mary's pot full with boiling soup in a cloud of smoke and vapor as it ran wailing in pain back to the forest.

So the family life was saved again due to a Divine intervention, but divinity left only a few spoons of soup, baked potatoes and eggs for the celebration as they started on the road to the capital city of the Vienna suburb called Treis Kirchen, (The three churches), where the majority of political refugees from the Iron Curtain were placed after being debriefed, health inspected, and checked by police and consular officials.

Father Emo had two days of meetings with intelligence officials, during which he was interrogated about details of his life so personal and precise that at times he was frightened how someone he had never seen before and so far from home could know so much about him. But it was all part of the procedure designed to make sure that he was who he claimed to be in order to receive a political asylum in some 50 countries, signatories of the 1954 Political Refugee Treaty.

Then there were a few weeks of strange silence, emptiness, and no activity at all that gave the family time to reflect on their newly won freedom, practice their German language, and start learning some English. As people have said, there is nothing scarier than deafening silence after living through a horrifying storm.

But the new freedom did not stop tireless Father Emo from writing letters in six languages to émigrés and officials all over Europe who could perhaps shed some light on the fate of his brother-in-law Rangel, who had last been heard from in 1953 while in KGB custody.

He did not realize that many of his contacts were in fact sell-outs, ears of the furious KGB, and judging from the newspaper clippings shown to him by the authorities, the family were a bunch of traitors and American spies fortunate to slip away from justice of the Communist State, at least for the time being.

Father Emo brushed aside all fears and continued to press in his investigation, again not realizing that the magnificent capital city of Vienna was not only a crown jewel of European culture but also one of the most active and dangerous centers of international espionage activity in the world, a reality about to become evident very shortly.

He had contacted a émigré in the city of Trieste on the Adriatic coast of Italy, a godfather of his sister Elsa, who reportedly was a contract worker for the CIA and claimed to have information about the fate of Rangel.

One beautiful day, Father Emo gave Alex two envelopes with directions to deliver the thick one to the consular official in the US Embassy in Vienna, located in downtown, not far from the famed Cathedral of Saint Stephen, one of the most iconic and spiritual places in the old city. The other envelope was to be delivered to a émigré nearby who supposedly was to help find the fate of missing Uncle Rangel based on information to be obtained from a network of refuseniks actively working against the Communist Regime.

Full of excitement that he would finally be able to leave the gloomy grounds of the camp and spend some time in magnificent Vienna, with streets lined up with small stores and coffee shops where one could see some of the most beautiful girls in world, Alex found himself in what seemed like minutes in downtown Saint Stephen Square, even though the trip actually took over half an hour. In the old cathedral with its all-Divine magic and history, he bought the largest candle with his last shillings and prayed on his knees that the man with a shadow of living gold will extend his hands over the family and protect them from the evil communists.

Back on the street under bright fall sun, heart enlightened with hope and happiness, Alex could not help walking a few streets over to the Mozarthaus, where the great master had met in 1787 his admirer and devoted student Ludwig van Beethoven, the creator of some of the world's most beautiful music and father of Musical Romanticism.

To feel the spirit of God and two of his messengers on the same day can lift a person sky high, so he was back on the street full with people, smiling at any girl that would smile at him, when he felt a dull thumb on the back of the head. There was no one behind him, yet the feeling was too real to ignore.

"My God, the KGB again. How did they know I'll be here?" a violent thought flashed in his mind.

The best way to find out if one is being followed is to lazily walk in one direction, then suddenly turn around and start walking back. The first clown that changes direction, start picking their nose or looking at the moon is the tail.

The trick worked as usual, as a finely dressed couple suddenly started looking at a store window, confirming the event under observation was what in the vocabulary of the KGB is called bagging. The target is followed by a couple of agents, a car on the street and another two or three goons on the opposite side leading to a point where the victim is sprayed with a drug, tossed in the back of a car and back to the old country one goes, never to be heard from again.

"Gosh, I should be honored if they have sent so many people after me to get those envelopes. I have to give them a run for it," he thought.

Paying attention to the traffic behind him soon made it obvious a red Porsche Targa with two characters inside was part of the bag, and even though he could not discern the others across the street, it was time to show who was in charge in the area.

Alex, like everyone else in the family, was given a document by the authorities requiring immediate assistance from security officials in case of trouble, and looking around like if by a Divine design, there was an enormous police officer, Sergeant Schmidt, leaning on a blue BMW, observing the street.

The man was dumbfounded when told someone was following Alex.

"Who and where are they?" he asked in disbelief.

The traffic was stopped, and the two walked to the red Porsche. It turned out to be a car of the Czechoslovakian Embassy and due to diplomatic immunity could not be searched nor the identities of the driver and passenger determined. A joint operation, as the KGB would say, indicating the danger was extreme, and with contacts like those Father Emo had, one hardly needed enemies.

Back at the police BMW, Alex pointed to the couple that had been tailing him for a while, but they vanished as soon they saw the police walking towards them.

Sergeant Schmidt was concerned.

"I will have a car drop you next to the

Embassy since it may be very dangerous to walk alone all the way up there."

"One cannot express in any way the appreciation of the professionalism and the integrity of the Austrian Police and Security Authorities," Alex told the officer, who dropped him a few streets from the Embassy.

"Thank you. Thank you very much."

There was a cobblestone-covered lonely street to cross, followed by a narrow strip park covered with acacia trees when he noticed to his left a young woman dressed in white, holding a bouquet of red tulips, her blue eyes beaming with light, her lips in a mysterious smile. Alex had already crossed the street, still looking at the woman, when he felt something like a bumble bee graze the back of his head and a shower of tree bark splashing over his face.

"My God, the KGB again, they found me again."

He fell on the ground, and there was another splash of tree bark all over as he crawled on his bloodied elbows through the park, fighting for dear life. A screeching of brakes and the sound of someone running toward him ended the terror. A police car had been just across the street and saw him running toward them.

Alex was dropped right in front of the Embassy until a windowless van came to pick him up and drive straight to the camp. The next day, the family was taken about 120 kilometers west in the mountains above the city of Linz to a small village called Grain, where a three-story building was housing families facing special security threats.

This was another place where refugees

were back to the deafening silence and boredom that can test the resolve of even the toughest person, resolve one can maintain only by walking around the pine tree-lined mountain roads to some of the historical landmarks, hoping to get one's mind away from the terror and danger of the past.

The rich cultural traditions and proud imperial past were evident everywhere, even in the smallest villages nestled at the base of the magnificent shadow of the Alps, with their snow-covered mountain tops and splendid and mysterious pine forest. Yet this was a country of many shades and contradictions, the most intriguing being the fact that on one side of the mountain, the city of Salzburg gave the world Wolfgang Amadeus Mozart, probably the greatest composer of all time, and the other side of the mountain, in the city of Braunou, Germany's Fuehrer Adolph Hitler, almost certainly the world's greatest war criminal.

Alex had heard a lot about the persecution and murder of millions of Jews during the Holocaust but never understood how a country like Austria could be the birthplace of anti-Semitism and aggression that almost destroyed the world.

The camp electrician, Willy, once a Hitler Youth member himself, put it in very plain terms.

"Look at all these villages up on the mountains. They were all for Hitler until the last moment the Russians came. You have to start coming with me to my service calls and even to Salzburg one day so that I can introduce you to some of these guys, and you can see for yourself whom you are up against. Don't tell anyone you're a student of the Holocaust, just say you are interested in war stories."

And war stories they were, and after every meeting with the veterans, and observing their meticulously preserved uniforms with all decorations in place and no sign of remorse after all these fateful years, Alex started getting chills in his timbers and the feeling that he had been following the footsteps of an ugly and bloody monster.

"Now comes the best part," Willy said jokingly.

"We are going to Salzburg this Thursday, and I am going to introduce you to some real characters."

The flea and farmers market was not far from Mozart's house, teeming with people eager to sell the magnificent fruits and vegetables they have hauled down from their farms.

"Do you see the old gentleman there on the right? This is Herr Erlenmeyer. Approach him, making sure the police are not around, raise your right arm and say, 'Hail Hitler.'"

"Hail Hitler, Comrade," Herr Erlenmeyer replied.

"How are you? Are you doing well?"

"Very good, thanks," Alex replied, almost running out of breath.

"May the Lord have a mercy on us all Willy, why are these people still saying "Hail Hitler" in 1969? This is very scary and disturbing."

Alex could not even imagine that another confrontation with the Nazi Germany's past was about to challenge him in his newly adopted country.

After four months in the mountains, the family was driven back to Vienna for an interview with the consular officials. A man with spectacle glasses who could have been the twin brother of

CIA Director Bill Casey, was very frank: "Our Americans are messed up. Tell anyone who cares to listen what you have seen and been through. And good luck in America."

Then the big day came on May 5, 1970. The family was driven to Vienna flughafen, boarding a silver Boeing 707, destination New York, USA. As the plane accelerated and the Austrian forest and mountains disappeared in the haze below, tears started flowing as everyone was overcome by emotion, feeling instinctively that the Providence was sending them to a place and a future from which there was no point of return, the first of the extended family to live and die on the North American continent and possibly never see Europe again.

Flying over the blue Atlantic seem to last forever until the Boeing finally changed direction and gently started descending southward as the coast and the impressive New York skyline became visible under the cover of scattered white, puffy clouds. Once on the tarmac, Father Emo could not help but kneel down and kiss the ground.

"Thank you Lord, thank you very much for leading us away from the evil of the Communists and to these blessed shores," he whispered in tears as a group of passengers respectfully looked on.

Arriving at Hopkins Airport in Cleveland and being driven to their rental house by a member of the support group IRC was the beginning of another journey into the familiar emptiness following the emotional storm of living through momentous events, just to be terrified by the deafening silence that followed.

Chapter 2

Ohio, the heart of it all

Finding yourself in a new country, not knowing the language, without much money, friends or any family support turned out to be much more difficult than anyone expected.

Since Alex couldn't speak English, the only place he could find a job was the docks of the Goodwill Industries as a truck helper. A majority of the workers on the docks were blacks, not friendly to white people just arriving from the boat and certainly not great admirers of any foreign language.

"In America you never admit to making a mistake and always say you are from German-Irish descent," advised the supervisor Clint McCloskey as Alex was given an hourly rate of 39 cents per hour because his ability to speak English was considered on a level of mental retardation. He was assigned to work with a charming Jamaican driver and retired Army sergeant called Pino the Vino because he liked to drink.

Pino and Alex scoured the neighborhoods and collected old dishwashers, refrigerators and other items donated by the good people of Ohio and then went back to the docks to unload their riches.

"Pino, are you really a person from German-Irish descent who never made a mistake in his life?" Alex would joke as they took to the roads of Ohio.

"Do I look like German to you, bro? Black German that will be the day. Don't listen to this idiot McCloskey and all his wisdom. My father was

100-percent Italian, and my dear mother was from Jamaica, so I make every mistake possible, and on Friday I get drunk like a log, including getting in jail for a few days."

Pino had an excellent voice and while driving would sing some Jamaican favorites, including Belafonte hits like "The Banana Song" with Alex in tow. As people have said, if you can sing a language, you can speak it, so eventually Alex started speaking some rudimentary English with a Jamaican accent.

The most exciting part of all these trips was the time when Pino would stop his truck in the middle of the ghetto to have a word with his friends and perhaps let them share some of the items in the truck. To find yourself surrounded by a group of 100 loud black men and women was a very scary experience for a young man from Bulgaria who had never seen a black person in his life. But he soon noticed that the African-Americans were good at heart and very polite, and in a couple weeks, he found himself with new friends who actually wanted to learn some Russian and were very interested in his story.

This new cultural fusion became noticeable to the Goodwill supervisor Jim Jones (a Sidney Poitier impersonator and another charming Jamaican), who decided that Alex was reasonably intelligent and a good worker worth of 59 cents an hour.

In one of these trips in the larger Akron-Canton area, Pino pulled abruptly into the driveway of an old, two-story gray house, nestled in the shadow of the Goodrich Tire Plant. There were six black men, sitting on chairs in a circle, reading and reciting from a Russian book one had borrowed from the library.

Usually jolly and lighthearted, Pino was clearly not amused by the gathering.

"Would you please tell these fools where you are coming from and why, in Russian please?"

The six were absolutely stunned to hear someone speaking crystal-clear Russian and explaining things they had heard about the Iron Curtain.

"Will the Russians let us free when they come to America?" one young lad asked.

"You are free fools, just try to learn good English and get decent jobs, instead of wasting time with these Russky commies," Pino growled.

"I spent years in Germany watching the fence and seeing people getting shot just for trying to get out to freedom."

To see a group of black men not enamored with how things were going in America was not new for Alex, especially on the docks of Goodwill Industries where a lot of them had left the Deep South to escape harassment and the violence of the Klan.

There was an older black man, whom everybody called Benny Ben (also known as Archibald Clemons), who was the wisdom and conscience of the docks, the man whom everyone wanted to talk to in times of trouble or hurt. Benny was so old that his eyes were blue and face cracked by the winds and trials of time, yet his deep and chanting voice sounded surprisingly young, matching a quick wit and broad sense of the human ways.

Benny's family left Mississippi at the beginning of century after the Klan had burned their house, finally setting roots and raising a family in Northeastern Ohio.

Still, the South was on his mind, and he would start humming from time to time old spirituals his mom sang in the church down in Tupelo, songs as old as America and touching like the holy prayer.

Alex had played the piano for years and was familiar with most modern music, yet the songs of Benny and the guys on the docks were as spiritual in conversation as in music and rhythm, like a living being talking to God in sound and prayer, music he had never heard before, music that no one had ever written. So he tried to pronounce the words as Benny did, clap his hands when Benny did and sing the blues as it was sung down south.

Every day at quarter past three, Benny would get an old shoe, start banging on the table, and sing, "Time to see my honey" and a hundred or so would reply, "Time to see my honey."

"Time to spend my money," and a hundred would repeat, "time to spend my money."

At that time the supervisor Jim Jones would show up and mock Benny, singing, "Knock it off, my honey, or I'll take your money."

The answer was usually, "Jim Jones… Jim Jones Jim Jones… Pim Pom Pim Pom."

The blacks could not pronounce "Ping Pong," and they did not like how Jones' supervisor's girlfriend, "the white bitch Sarah" as they called her, was ping-ponging him (running him around).

One day Pino brought in a large older model electric organ, a gift from a church in the area. Alex was tempted to try it out during the break and put some blues harmonies, a back up to Benny's songs.

As Alex was trying to keep up, Benny all of sudden switched to "Let's praise the Lord" with the harmony and rhythm of a full orchestra. All of the guys started singing, clapping their hands and dancing like they did during Sunday service in the South Hawking Baptist Church.

The usually gray docks filled with old furniture and tired and sometimes depressed people have been lit by the music, faces glowing, auras of the most beautiful colors of the spectrum, the halls filled with sound of voices that had sung this music during the darkest days of slavery and oppression down south, when the Church and faith were the only places to seek shelter.

Alex had found the key to the hearts of the African Americans. Their music was the living blood and body of the community, the language every one of them understood and felt.

When everything was said and done with Benny's song, innumerable hands, embraces and taps on the back let Alex know he was now part of the African-American family. He has been promoted from a "mama lie" to a "honky mother fucker" to a "honky" to a "brother."

Benny Ben and his sidekick Cornelius Brown, also known as Corky, soon gave Alex his first lesson in American political philosophy when they introduced him to the definition of the "Republican part of Heaven."

"Heaven is 95 percent Democrats, 5 percent Republicans and 15 percent other motherfuckers," Corky would joke.

"On the other hand, Hell is 99 percent Republicans and 5 percent former Klansmen."

"Don't listen to him; his percent's are faulty," Benny would holler.

"Shut up you old man, don't you know God has no percentages? I knows he doesn't."

According to Benny, Republican was a "Klan mama lie with a fine haircut, perfect leather shoes owning an Insurance Agency."

"You see," Benny would say, "all troubles in America come from the white people's politicians. It would be very nice for the country if they could spend one weekend a month in jail with the rest of us."

"They start wars; raise your taxes and burn down houses of black people."

"You ain't never seen a black man starting a war, have you?"

"White people politicians are the world's biggest motherfuckers I say."

"And GOP, meaning Gray Orangutan Party," Corky snapped acidly.

"Shut up now Corky, don't you confuse my student man."

"There is always a "Third Hand" with them, always."

"But I feel offended when you call the white people all these bad things," Alex protested.

"You ain't no white person if you is with us, bro. You are simply a white slave."

"But calling black people names is terribly offending, don't you think Ben? I was told never to use that word."

"I ain't no race police bro. My people came from the River Niger parts in Africa so I don't mind the name one bit, do I?"

"Black people feel the hate of the words, not the words themselves, you hear? You are one of us, and we take you with our hearts, not words."

Alex thought for many years that calling the

American politicians "motherfuckers" was one of the less successful wisdoms of Benny Ben. But after observing the American landscape for forty years and having voted in many elections, it became evident that Benny's observation about the "Third Hand" in American Politics was the understatement of the century, to say the least. Some twenty years after this conversation, a Majority Leader, a Republican and Presidential candidate, a Democrat, sworn enemies on the evening TV shows, were actually both members of the Trilateral Commission. How an uneducated black man could deduce such complex political events was a mystery, but it was becoming very clear that the boundless wisdom, vision and resolve of the American People was coming from the ordinary folks down below, like a mountain stream gushing crystal clear water down the hill, sweeping everything in its way, not to surrender even to the biggest boulders and deepest canyons. The ordinary Americans were much more sophisticated and multidimensional people than he had ever imagined.

This was not the first time the family had encountered ill feelings and resentment toward the American system and especially the Vietnam War. Behind the old house on Center Street was the anti-war movement headquarters, which became particularly aggressive after the May 4, 1970 Kent State University shooting of student war protesters by the Ohio National Guard.

Every night, especially on Fridays, a large congregation of hippies would gather in and around the house with hippies on the balcony, hippies in the trees, hippies in the sky and the smell of marijuana all over the neighborhood to discuss the latest plans of how to get rid of his Imperial Majesty and America's Most Wanted Man, President Richard Millhouse Nixon. The hippies were a rowdy, drunk and disorganized commune. It was not unusual to hear someone's scream in the middle of the night, having caught on fire after falling asleep with a pot cigarette in their mouth and a beard soaked in whiskey.

One of the most enigmatic inhabitants of the commune was a young photographer, Rich Lymon, who had recently been drafted for Vietnam, only for the military to find out that due to his very bad vision, he was a greater threat to the American troops than Charlie and promptly excused from active service.

His artistic portfolio contained a wide and frank visual history of the turbulent period the country was going through, including some famous and faithful events with a definite bias for the offbeat and transcendental in the human experience.

Like most of the hippies, he was from a privileged background, son of a wealthy Canadian doctor and landowner who had left the family shortly after his birth and an American mother, an employee of the State Department of Taxation.

The betrayal of his father left Rich hurt, lonely and confused, so after attending a prestigious military academy and being rejected for active duty, he poured all his soul and gifts into creating a record of the anti-war movement and in the daily chores of the committee against the war.

For someone who recently crossed the Iron Curtain at great peril and a personal witness of the communist terror, it was quite strange to see groups of young, highly educated and good-looking young Americans from well-to-do families act hostile toward their own government to the point of rebellion and mutiny and eagerness to take to the streets at the shortest notice.

It did not take long for the most curious hippies to ask the question that was on their mind.

"How will we be treated behind the Iron Curtain if we take to the streets against Khrushchev?"

"You will be lucky to end up in a labor camp where your long greasy hair and beards will be shaved, and then sent to the frozen fields to dig turnips out of the ground with your bare hands," Alex replied.

"And if we refuse?"

"You'll be conveniently shot in the back for trying to escape."

The hippies did not appreciate the comment but after a few days offered Alex a marijuana cigarette and invited him to join the Friday night party, which he politely refused. This was the end of their relationship for the time being.

Not much later, Alex had a run-in with a Communist cell of six students based in Columbus, who were most eager to hear a firsthand account of how the miracles of communist heaven were about to change the world. They were so indoctrinated in the belief that the writings of Marx and Lenin would lead to a new and higher social order that they started their weekly meetings singing the revolutionary workers hymn, "Forward to victory, folks, the red banner will triumph."

The students did not understand how deeply the early Communist theory was influenced by the eastern religions with limited doctrine of mercy such as Islam, where Muslims would pray to

Lord Mohammed the Magnificent, God and Son of God, whereby the communist who did not believe in God would worship some ruthless and disgusting peasant who had managed to climb to the top of the party hierarchy on a mountain of bodies of refuseniks in the infamous labor camps. Yet the Muslim clerics called all gentiles "Kafir" or infidels, as the KGB officers liked to remind their victims, "You are with or against us," which is basically the same joke.

The story awaiting American communists was not pretty at all. During the Red Terror of Stalin and his henchman Laurenty Beria, the family had been interned for eight years to the Northern Bulgaria's village of Tervel, a place where the winters were so severe that one cannot only hear the words but actually see them. In fact, one of Alex's earliest memories was when he and his brother Ted were filling a brick form with mud with their small hands, trying to help Mother Mary and Father Emo build the two-room shack during the summer of 1951, a shack whose roof and the whole northern side would level with the snow in the winter.

There was a large, gloomy cement KGB building in the center of the village where the nearby stone wall of an old school was a place the children would climb up and observe prisoners being tortured and abused daily.

The KGB was of course the world-premier expert in beating handcuffed people. One of Alex's most frightful memories was the view of a prisoner whose hands and legs were spread using four ropes, his body slowly lowered to a rope crushing his genitals.

The scream was not heard, but the terror

and pain on this man's face was deeply imprinted forever in his young mind.

The American Communists were shocked.

"You mean they really did that? This is unbelievable."

There was more bad news. The KGB was beating their most ardent enemies with long, thin bags filled with sand, which would not leave many skin marks but lead to internal injuries, causing prisoners to spit or excrete blood, then releasing them to die at home.

Father Emo, an attorney speaking eleven foreign languages, was outraged.

"The brutality of this people is such that no man of conscience can stand still. I said the same thing about the Nazi persecution of the Jews years ago."

And he did not stand still. He wrote a letter in French to the Red Cross in Switzerland, and every month, a hundred or so big red penicillin pills would arrive at a common mailbox at the bus station. Father Emo and Alex would then walk around town followed by a KGB agent to the houses of the people dying from internal injuries, then making a sharp turn to distract his tail while Alex would sneak in and deliver ten pills to the family.

Hundreds of people were saved from almost certain death to the fury of the KGB, who in turn would take some of the prisoners back with no avail. No one ever talked.

The desolation of the village was such that it would take weeks for common news to reach the people. In 1951, Alex and Ted started building a rudimentary linear receiver using a diagram from a popular Soviet radio amateur magazine with the antenna stretched between two 12-foot poles, 40 feet apart, using a pair of enormous WWII earphones and producing the variable capacitor by cutting slices of thin cans.

With the radio all done, Ted moved the detector needle in the piece of ore used as a diode, put the earphones on, and tenderly moved the flimsy variable capacitor from left to right in search of a station. There was a hiss, followed by a long stretch of static noise, then the beautiful sound of Celeste playing the Carillon melody "Christus Vincit" many times, followed by a male voice announcing, "This is Radio Vatican."

The family was frantic. This was a voice from far away, free from the terror of the KGB, a voice of reason and hope, not afraid to speak the truth or pray to the Lord.

After a couple days, there was even greater victory; Alex was able to catch the broadcast of the Voice of America, which always started with "Columbia, the Gem of the Ocean," followed by the day's news.

The KGB was not amused, having been alerted by the goon across the street who was always hiding under the back window of the house, listening to all conversations inside. The radio was confiscated and a long list of charges leveled against Father Emo and the children, starting with "Possession of illegal transmitter radio in order to get in touch with the dark forces of the CIA."

But then even people as stupid as the KGB realized that this was a receiver, built using a Soviet diagram published in Moscow, so the radio was returned and the matter forgotten for the time being.

"You cannot believe how fortunate you are

to be Americans," Father Emo told the students.

"Stop betraying this great country with your service to the Communists. You are walking in the bloody footsteps of an indescribable evil, and please think about these poor men and all other victims of the Red Terror before spending a dime on these people, if you can call them that."

Some American Communists left frightened and disillusioned.

"We are sorry for what you have suffered," one of the girls told Father Emo.

"I will tell all my friends about you."

"We are proud that your humanity was recognized by the political asylum granted in some 50 countries around the world."

Most of the more fanatical and brainwashed members of the group left unimpressed and hostile after starting an ideological fight on how the theory of Marx, Engels and Lenin will transform America into a brotherhood of men, all equal to share the bounty of the State. They simply refused to accept how inefficient the communist system was and that only the private enterprise based on personal interest had been successful in providing endless supplies of goods and services to its citizens.

Still, when Father Emo passed away in 1997, out of the fifty-some hippies and communists who gathered behind the old house on Center Street, only one came to the funeral. They never forgave him for speaking the truth in 1970.

Rich Lymon was the only one who forgave him.

The first Christmas in America was strangely silent and painful since it had been more than 20 years the family celebrated the holy day in the open in fear of persecution from the KGB.

This was the time the brothers had acquired a car from the Calabrese clan across the street, a 1966 Fiat that was traded for a Zenith color television, two freshly baked loaves of bread and a bowl of unbelievably tasty pasta "al dente" made by Mrs. Testa.

The car had no brakes at all, but after some work it was on the road, ready to explore the vastness of Ohio. Only two passengers could ride at a time since it was so small that going through a pothole at a high speed or taking a deep breath could be a quite an experience, especially to people with broad lines.

One day in early December 1970, a faint cry made Alex open the front door, only to see a small kitten on the snow-covered porch, so he could not help but tenderly lift her and take her in. She was hungry, very hungry, and was treated with warm milk and a little cat food. When she looked him in the eyes, he fell instantly in love since she had the most beautiful green eyes in the world and being so small, he decided to call her Mini.

Cleaned and spayed the next day, Mini was an early Christmas gift to the family, as everyone liked to hold her tenderly, share some tasty foods with her, or simply take a nap with her little heart beating nearby.

The day before Christmas, Alex had to do a little shopping but she wanted to come also, so he could not resist putting her in his coat with just her head with two big green eyes showing behind the zipper. She had to stay in the Fiat in the parking lot, and when he was done and ready to go back with Mini in the warm coat, Alex saw an old lady, scantily dressed, arms red from the cold, pushing her cart through the snow-covered parking lot in a freezing wind and drizzle. He immediately recognized her as Mrs. Gromsky who was living alone in an apartment over the drug store on Maple Square. He stopped the car and offered to take her home if she would hold Mini to which she agreed, and soon they were back at her apartment with all groceries in place. Mini curiously explored the new frontier, but did not yet allow herself to be held by this unknown person.

That very night, Alex had a dream that he was in a big metal cage and saw Christ, the same Christ he had been blessed to see back in the Old Country. Christ came, opened the cage door, and handed him a large, shining cross. He took this as a sign that every Christmas something must be done to help those alone or in need, a good work he continued to do for many years to come.

Meanwhile, his sister Talia had started dating an enigmatic Canadian engineering student Tony Piazza, whose father had emigrated from Sicily at the end of the war. Alex would let them borrow the Fiat for their excursions and with special permission take Mini, with whom they both had fallen in love at first sight. The definition of a Sicilian according to Tony Piazza, was an Italian person who carried a submachine gun in a violin case and a roll of piano wire in the pocket, a joke that brought a cloud of suspicion and mistrust in the eyes of Mother Mary. But the Piazzas turned out to be another close-knit, hard-working Italian clan, so Tony was warmly accepted as a new addition to the family after an old-world wedding in Toronto with many flowers, beautiful Italian canzonets and mandolin music, which brought tears to the eyes of over 300 attendants.

The happy days at the docks of Goodwill Industries came to an end when Mr. Harlan Wineright, a friend of Father Emo, came to the house one evening.

"I will pick you up at nine in the morning and introduce you to an important businessman," he whispered mysteriously.

What Alex did not realize at the time was that he was leaving the colorful world of the African-Americans and re-entering the cold and hostile domain of the Nazis, the very same Nazis he started studying in Austria.

Chapter 3

The Germans

Working for Panser Electronics was Alex's
first real job, a job he landed due the fact that he
spoke German and had educational background in
electrical and electronic circuits.

It was an enormous cultural transition for
him. The most startling thing about working with
Mr. Panser was his blatant anti-Semitism and
racism. Rudolf Panser (Mr. Pansy), as his Russian
Front comrades called him, was born in a small
village near Weimar, Germany, joining the Hitler
Youth and the Nazi Party in his twenties. This was
a memorable engagement that took him all the way
to Stalingrad, where he spent two unforgettable
years serving in the Wehrmacht Signal Corp
installing telephone links, many times under
vicious Russian bombardment. All the men in
Rudolf's unit were fortunate to have a wise and
caring commanding officer, Col. Lemke, who had
the strange premonition of sensing the forthcoming
Russian attacks and the courage to pull his soldiers
back from the doomed area.

On the personal side, the best thing that
happened to him in Russia was a Folk Deutsche
girl named Ingrid who followed him during the
retreat back to Germany. The Russians were
shooting relentlessly as the Germans were
retreating to the Reich, until finally he was
captured by the American troops, sobbing
uncontrollably. Rudolf married his sweetheart and
immigrated to the United States with help from
some of his Wehrmacht comrades already in
Canton, Ohio where he started a small electronics

business.

Soon, all of the men of his unit that were fortunate enough to come back from Russia made their way to America, including his childhood friend Bruno Hessler, a decorated Luftwaffe pilot who flew a Heinkel bomber in the Battle of Britain.

In one of his raids to Britain, a hit by an ack-ack shell sparked fire on board and caused injuries to the crew. He managed to land the aircraft but suffered serious damage to his right leg, which left him with a limp that some of his friends jokingly referred to as "Das Georing" limp. To give the Luftwaffe credit, Bruno could not stand the Nazis and had frequent heated arguments with Mr. Panser regarding their crimes during the European conflict. Alex was astonished to find out that even though the war was long over, many Germans were still expecting the inevitable return of a racial struggle in which all Jews and other colored people "will be stoned on the streets by the new all-white American Reich."

An exalted, New World greeting was awaiting him.

"Alex, you look like a goddamn Jew and your days are numbered. Soon we will chase all the Jews off the streets," Mr. Panser looked sternly at the young man who had been his employee for hardly two days.

"Such an arrogant statement," Alex thought.

"Hitler is gone, the Gestapo is gone. Who is 'we,' Rudy?" he asked aloud.

"We are the new force that will sweep the world, and you will be one of the first to feel it together with the blacks," Mr. Panser snapped.

"But Rudy, you look yourself like an Orthodox Rabbi," Alex quipped.

"Just put the black hat on, grow a beard and go praying to the Wailing Wall. You may be one of the first to be swept to the concentration camps with your African-American friends."

The brutality of this argument shocked Mr. Panser so much that he pulled in front of the mirror and took a long, worried look at his face.

"He really looks like an Orthodox Jew, and I have been telling him this since childhood," Bruno Hessler added jokingly.

"I always wondered if his real family name might be Rudolf Panser-Rabinovitz."

"Perhaps some Jewish relatives in the not-so-distant past, aye Pansy? Wasn't your Grandpa Helmuth a tailor in Berlin? I know for sure that most tailors in Berlin were Jews. You're not hiding your Zionist roots, are you?" Bruno retorted.

"Shut up, you Luftwaffe clown!" Mr. Panser exploded.

"If your fat blob commander and miserable pilots had defended Germany, we would not be in this position."

"I certainly did not surrender to anyone, like some people in this room," Bruno countered.

"I simply took off my flying jacket with all decorations on it and went home with my head up."

"Besides, you and your dear Wehrmacht friends are much better off here than back east, all very fortunate to have saved your miserable hide from the Russians."

As they say, the wolf changes his fur but not the habits.

To this end, Rudolf had equipped his truck

43

console with a self-defense rack, including an enormous German Luger always ready to shoot at the Jews, cast-iron baton called the "Gestapo" pipe and other weapons, all prominently displayed.

Out of all tools of mass destruction in Mr. Panser's arsenal, the "Gestapo" pipe was the one that horrified Alex the most. Rudolf and his Ukrainian brother-in-law Ivan had taken an 18 by half-inch cast-iron pipe, filled it up with sand, put end caps, and attached a hand strap, making it weigh in excess of two pounds.

"Rudolf, in the mind of a cultured person, the usage of this pipe must be a war crime," Alex complained.

"How can a person coming from Germany, with all your culture and tradition, hit another human being in the head with a 18-inch cast iron pipe? This is a Nibelungean barbarity."

"Alex, you're a dumb foreigner and have no idea how thick the skulls of the blacks are," Mr. Panser growled.

"You will learn better one of these days when they rob you at gunpoint and beat the shit out of you in some small alley."

"You wouldn't hit a white person with the 'Gestapo' pipe, would you, Rudy?" Alex continued.

"Of course not," Mr. Pansy replied.

"I like to be very nice to stupid white people. That's why I carry the baseball bat and the dog spray in the back of the truck."

The African Americans were of course aware that Mr. Panser did not like them, and even though his friendship with South Cayley Street Baptist Church Most Reverend Jim West was well known, one could often see few teens marching in front of the store with their right hand extended (thumb down) in a Nazi salute, chanting "Hail Pansy, Sig Hail."

So it did not take long for passions to boil over in the July heat as one morning, the back window of the store was broken and a large brick with a swastika inscribed on it found on the floor.

The glass blocks were promptly replaced and everyone conveniently assumed that the incident was a random act of violence, until the next day when the window got busted again.

This was clearly an act of impending hostilities in Mr. Panser's suspicious mind, so a war council was convened, consisting of himself and his brother-in-law Ivan, in order to deal with the African-American partisans and apply some of the tactics the Wehrmacht had used in Russia.

First, an infrared sensor was installed in the backyard to warn of hostile intrusions by triggering a silent alarm designed to give the person on watch enough time to at least grab the Gestapo pipe or the handgun.

Second, a large opening was bored in the back door to attach a swivel, making the barrel of Mr. Panser's Luger protrude out with sufficient field of fire in case things escalated into a full-blown firefight.

The next thing was simply to wait for the blacks to make their move.

Despite all German precision and war planning, one thing omitted was the realization that the African-American partisans were an intelligent and stealthy enemy, more dangerous even than the Russians and completely unpredictable.

So as Ivan had taken his turn to guard the store in the wee hours of the night and Pansy has fallen asleep in the service room, the soft silence of the summer night was all of a sudden shattered by gunfire.

Someone was firing the Luger, and to the absolute horror of Mr. Panser, the gun appeared to fire by itself.

The back door was opened, and it was found that while Ivan has snoozed off (which he vehemently denied), someone had crawled under the infrared sensor, tied a noose on the tip of the barrel of the Luger and then tied the string to the doorknob of the neighboring business.

Another noose was hooked to the gun trigger, so the partisans were able to fire from a distance of at least 10 feet.

"Brilliant, absolutely brilliant," Bruno exclaimed in the morning with Alex nodding in agreement.

"You have to thank the Lord that the African American partisans were not at Stalingrad. May I suggest you start building some real suntan, listen to the blues and seriously consider changing your race classification from German to African American? These guys hold a lot of promise."

The rage of Mr. Pansy knew no bounds.

"You imbeciles, moron lovers," he screamed at Alex and Bruno.

"I will find the black son of bitch who did this and personally crack his thick skull with the Gestapo pipe. He got me in trouble with the police and put me into 117 dollars of expense to repair the neighbor's back door."

But as time passed, passions subsided and cooler heads prevailed as Mr.Pansy realized that his chances of revenge against the black resistance were none to nil, so the back window was quickly walled off and the whole matter soon forgotten.

On the Jewish front, there was another surprise.

One of Mr. Panser's customers was a Jewish lady, Olga Milstein. She was born somewhere in the vastness of west Russia, having spent most of her 34 years living in the small village of Belinka, a Jewish hamlet of some 14 houses huddled next to a large forest.

One summer day, while Olga and some other girls labored in the endless wheat fields of the local Kolkhoz, a unit of the Wehrmacht arrived in hot pursuit of a band of partisans who had just attacked a German convoy on the main road to Minsk.

A gun battle erupted, and when everything was done and gone, Belinka was no more, blown to pieces by the German guns, houses afire and dead bodies all around.

For Olga and her three friends, there was only one thing to do: run to the magic Russian forest, join the partisans, and avenge the massacre of Belinka. Olga enlisted in the Red Army and fought bravely all the way to Berlin, where she met an American soldier, Josh Milstein. It was a meeting meant to be, so she followed him to the American sector, requested and was granted an asylum. They married and moved to Ohio to stay with Josh's parents until they got their own house in Canton.

But the fact that she fought with the Nazis did not mean she would never face them again as Josh soon ran into Mr. Panser's business and became a customer.

The question of Belinka soon came to the attention of the people of Mr. Panser's unit and to his absolute astonishment, the Germans were deeply embarrassed and sorry about the senseless loss of life in Byelorussia and elsewhere in the East.

One day, Mr. Panser sent Alex to do a service call, fix her television set and check the electrical outlets of the house.

The crystal-clear Russian language of Alex brought a river of memories of her beloved country, beautiful Belinka and the host of family and friends that had fallen during the war. Olga's biggest hurt was the loss of her young son Volodia and husband Igor, so she started calling Alex by his name and talking to him like he was Igor.

Alex was heartbroken by her story and soon started coming to the house every Friday to help Olga buy groceries, cook food and clean up around the house.

During one of those visits, he was surprised to see two of Mr. Pansy's comrades helping Olga trim the bushes and cut the grass in front of the house.

"I cannot believe the Wehrmacht would be helping an old Jewish woman," Alex protested to Mr. Pansy.

"You sure these guys are Germans?"

"Very German," Mr. Pansy replied.

"They were with me at Stalingrad. We did a lot of bad things in Russia and owe this woman an apology; if one can apologize for killing a whole village in Russia."

"The Wehrmacht must be a great army if they have a conscience to apologize 30 years after the war for the wrongs they have done," Alex admitted to Bruno Hessler.

"Now all we have to do is arrange for a barbecue picnic with the local synagogue."

"I wouldn't expect too much from Mr. Gestapo 1970 and start dancing in the streets," Bruno warned.

"Just stand by and he'll start with that old song again."

It did not take long for Mr. Pansy to show how unapologetic he was regarding the Jewish question.

"We never had the time to get rid of these heimees back in Europe. Hopefully, we will have a better chance in the New World."

"Here we go again," Alex thought.

"This man is suffering from a terminal case of Nazi paranoia."

A devilish plan started to form in Alex's mind. He had recently met a charming Russian Rabbinical student named Victor, fresh off the boat with his wife Miriam and young daughter Lila. Alex briefed him on the outrageous behavior of Mr. Panser and was surprised that he wanted to meet him.

"You have to get rid of your Zionist clothes, shave your beard, comb your hair to look like a charming young man and definitely remove the yarmulke from your head," Alex advised.

"Or Mr. Pansy may lose his nerve and shoot you with the Luger or crack your head with the Gestapo pipe, making you Holocaust victim 6,000,001, and I will have no part of it."

So the anti-Pansy conspiracy was to work as follows: Victor was to stop by the store and casually meet Alex, who in turn would ask Mr. Panser to explain to him how to build an antenna for a shortwave radio set capable of hearing Russia.

To Alex's astonishment, the casual encounter between Mr. Panser and Victor ended up in a friendly hour and a half of conversation, and he was invited to have a beer with the Wehrmacht unit during the usual Friday night gathering in Lou's Tavern across the street.

The warm, sincere smile of Victor, his goodhearted humanity and beautiful Russian had all of a sudden made him comrade to the Germans, turning back the flow of time some 30 years, when they were young soldiers walking through the endless plains of Russia, caught in a deadly struggle with people who at the end they have learned to respect and admire.

All of the guys drank schnapps, sang "Lily Marlene" and "When the Soldiers March," then switched to vodka, sang "Katyusha" and even tried to dance some kazachok with their tired old legs.

It was a widely successful night, and Victor found 35 new friends and admirers.

Alex had very bad feelings about all this.

"Now Mr. Pansy will find out who Victor is, shoot him with the Luger, and it will be my fault, all my fault," he thought, looking in the mirror.

"Alex Chaikin, you are a troublemaker and conspirator, yes you are."

The end came fast and brutal.

Mr. Panser had stopped by the mall to buy a couple notebooks, while at the same time Victor, dressed in his usual Zionist clothes, was helping the local synagogue with their cookie and pastry sale.

Their eyes met, the hunter and the hunted, the Nazi and the Jew.

Mr. Panser said nothing, just turned around and left the mall.

The next day he missed work, complaining of headache and sleeplessness.

"This is the first time he skipped work in nineteen years," Bruno observed.

"Something serious must have happened."

The next day, Pansy was still absent.

"I am very concerned," Bruno admitted.

"He must be hearing the howling of the crowds during the Nuremberg rallies and Hess shouting, 'The Party is Germany, Hitler is the Party, and Hitler is Germany, Sieg Heil, Sieg Heil.'"

On the third day Mrs. Panser came to Alex with the bad news.

"He won't come back unless you leave. You must go, go now."

Alex took his tools and left the store, followed by Bruno who wore his Iron Cross.

"During the forty years I have known this man, no one, and I mean no one, had the courage to put him in his place. The Luftwaffe salutes you."

Walking down the street toward the South Cayley Street Baptist Church, Alex was still trying to comprehend the events of the last hour.

"On one hand I lost a $400 a month job. On other hand, I won the respect of a distinguished Lufwaffe pilot and tried to build a bridge between the Germans and the Jews. Was it worth $400? Probably."

Down the road, he bumped into Calvin Kelly, a small black man with a big, golden heart whom he had met during the happy days on the Goodwill docks.

Kelly was philosophical.

"Those goddamn Nazis brains are wicked and crazy, bro. You did good, you did right, don't worry. You can always find a new job, but you may not be able to right wrongs. I am proud of you."

Chapter 4

The Jews

"Anyone who had the decency and courage to start a fight with Rudolf Panser is a friend of mine. I simply cannot stand that man," Sol Henny warmly shook Alex's hand.

"Welcome to my business friend, I hope you feel at home with us."

So Alex had another page of his life unravel, leaving the docks of Goodwill and the simple humanity of the African Americans to enter the cold and hostile domain of Rudolph Panser, just to leave again and share the practical and honest world of an Orthodox Jew who happened to be one of the founders of the local synagogue.

Sol Henny, formally known as Solomon Heenstein, was quite a character of his own to be sure. Arriving at the age of 15 from his native Poland, having left his younger siblings with relatives due to the early passing of his parents, he found himself in the Roaring Twenties in a country full with life and excitement yet completely alone and with only few dollars in his pocket.

So what could a Jewish orphan do but to get with some shady characters and mule illegal booze for few dimes a day to make ends meet?

According to Henny, the Kennedy gang headed by the father of the future political dynasty had subsidiaries all over the Midwest, including the Akron-Canton area, pushing booze during the Prohibition and other illegal activities including drugs and prostitution.

Having the honest face of an East

European peasant had earned Sol the modest accomplishment of never being stopped by the police when carrying booze, a distinction that soon led to a job with the Kennedy gang.

Sol's new corporate position included hauling booze to Cleveland and other cities using the back roads of Ohio for the incredible pay of 10 dollars per week plus work expenses.

Even though Henny was involved in what one can call a less than religious occupation, his background in Judaism had kept him from getting mixed with the violence that very often accompanied gang activity, except his inexhaustible appetite for women.

At the age of 24, he made his first mistake in life and married a hotheaded, big-busted Irish woman. Wise people have said that "If your lower half rules, the upper half suffers," a truth Henny was about to discover the hard way himself. The Casanova leanings of Sol were plainly visible to the jealous Irish beauty and punches started flying as soon it became clear the five feet nine inches Henny was no fighting match for her fury.

So he ran away and then made his second great life mistake. Sol met Rachel, the beautiful daughter of a Rabbi in Canton, fresh from Russia, whose greatest and most cherished dream was to establish a synagogue in the area so that the growing Jewish community in Ohio would have a rock to lean on and God to pray to. Henny was not particularly interested in the Rabbi's dreams, but the daughter caught his hungry eyes. It was "The Call of Judaism," as he was joking later.

But there was a problem. How could a bum like Sol Henny, working for the Kennedy gang pushing booze, convince the daughter of an

Orthodox Rabbi that he was living to the highest orders and ideals of the Judaism?

Sol had to hold his fire in a very long courtship until suspicious Rachel and the family was finally convinced that he was simply an old-fashioned Jewish orphan longing to have a family in the best traditions of the Jewish fate.

The late twenties found Henny with an obedient and loving wife, two sons, and all the gold he had saved during his years as an associate of the Kennedy gang. As some of his hoodlum friends started investing their money into more respectable circles of society such as politics and the stock market, the enterprising brain of Sol had a vision: buy a small, profitable electric business with established workforce and good, modern prospects and join the good life of the respected people.

In the twenties, there was no bigger fad than radio and electricity, and since Henny had never been to school in his life, it was time to take some courses, start reading books and complete his high school education so he could keep up with his workers and the business.

Everything was going so well in his life that the street-smart Sol was beginning to wonder if the Lord of the Jews was warning him about a bad joke waiting to reveal itself just around the corner.

Encouraged by his Rabbi father-in-law, he became thrifty and careful and stayed away from the stock market.

When the 1929 crash came, Henny already knew what the joke was, but a lot of his highflying customers were not so lucky, losing in a matter of months what they had earned in a lifetime.

Since people are creatures of habit and not necessarily reason, Casanova Henny again started fooling around with some of the characters of his not-so-distant past.

As people say, we first smell the rose and then get pricked by the thorns.

Rachel immediately noticed his indiscretions, and punches started flying even more furiously than with the Irish woman, Sol again playing the role of the punching bag. The problem this time was that he could not divorce an Orthodox Jewish woman, and so all fights were eventually settled in bed after Sol swore in the Holy Book of Torah that he would never even look at another woman in his life, (at least for the time being).

As the crash threw the whole world into a tailspin, Henny found himself the proud owner of a business without any orders; in fact, without any future. Then he remembered some of his hoodlum friends, who as pillars of the community had now branched into the political and business circles, so he made a few calls to see if he could get some government contract or any job at all and save his company. The contract he did get, and the favor wasn't cheap at all, but Sol was able to sail through the difficult years until the re-arming of America and President Roosevelt's New Deal started taking hold of the country. The best and certainly the most profitable advice he got from his bootlegger friends was to buy 10,000 shares of a major Hollywood company stock right at the bottom of the market at about 15 cents a share. After all the splits and dividends, re-investments were worth nearly $2 million in 1970.

In the 1930s, Henny was also watching with great suspicion and fear the rise of a nondescript Austrian house painter named Adolf Hitler to the position of the Reich Chancellor of Germany, which made him think of providing a set of Panamanian passports to his relatives in Poland. The Panamanian passports turned out to be a godsend since his folks were able to slip out of Poland just before the spring of 1939 and then into Bulgaria, from where they took the boat to Palestine.

Unfortunately, being a Jew surrounded by hostile Arabs in the 1930s Middle East was definitely not fun and continued to be so even after the state of Israel was founded in 1948. Henny found himself to be by default an early supporter of the Jewish State.

By that time, his father-in-law had founded the South Perkins Street Synagogue and Henny was appointed senior trustee and the chairman of the investment and recovery committee.

The end of the war produced a flood of refugees in America including thousands of Jews, some of which were Holocaust survivors, creating enormous strain on the resources of all the rescue organizations, including the synagogue. According to Henny, a member of the synagogue could borrow up to seven times his capital before he could give up on a start-up business, and once successful, must pool capital to support other businesses; an arrangement that was clearly the base of the Jewish economic power.

It took years for the community to rebuild and grow roots in America, so by the time Alex arrived in Henny's business, he was quite amazed by the glitter and glory of the Jewish social life. The people in the Synagogue warmly accepted Alex in their community once they heard where he was coming from, after all there were many great countries in Europe, but only the civilized Bulgaria had sheltered and protected the Jews from the Nazi terror.

So every business day, Henny and Alex did the rounds all over the Akron-Canton area and along the way would provide service to many members of the synagogue, also keeping an eye on the houses of members who were away on vacation or perhaps in the hospital.

On one such a day, Henny stopped his Dodge van in front of a majestic, brick Tudor house, handed the keys to Alex and sent him in to check if everything was all right.

When Alex got into the house, he saw something he wished to never have seen; the whole first floor was ransacked. All the pictures on the top of the fireplace were knocked down to the floor, the old menorah candles crushed with a brick and a sign on the wall, "Jew, get out soon."

When Henny came inside to inspect the damage, he couldn't believe how infuriated Alex was.

"This is the same hatred, the same goddamn Nazi hatred I saw in Austria. How long will you Jews put up with this shit? Allow me to hide in the closet with a baseball bat in hand, so I can catch the son of a bitch who did this and personally beat the crap out of him"

"You will do no such thing," Henny ordered.

"We don't want any violence or a scene. This is probably a dumb kid having some fun. Lock the door, get out, and let me handle it. I will notify the police and let them investigate this outrage."

Even though Alex was impressed by the

57

civility and patience of Henny, this matter did not go away peacefully. After a few weeks, he was back in the same house to deliver a new radio to the owner. Hardly five minutes had passed after entering the house when Alex heard the door lock click and someone walking like a cat into the foyer.

The only weapon he could grab in time was the fireplace fork, rushing into the living room screaming, "Drop to the ground or you are dead!"

It was a kid, a 12-or 13-year-old black boy holding a brick and fortunately, no gun.

"Drop the brick or I'll crack you head open," Alex said.

The brick went down.

"Please sir, don't kill me, please don't," the boy cried.

"I was just trying to get few dollars, just a few dollars."

"This kid is skinnier than a broomstick, and if I hit him, I wouldn't be better than Mr. Panser, would I?" Alex thought.

A diplomatic approach was clearly needed.

"What's your name, kid? What in the world are you doing in this man's house holding a brick?"

"I is Rodney Brown, and my uncle Tyrone Wang gave me two dollars to come in and break a few things. Please don't kill me for this, please. I just got the door key from under the floor mat and got in."

"It is dumb, very stupid to leave the house keys under the front door floor mat," Alex thought for himself.

It was time to lay down the law.

"Listen to me kid, and listen very good. You go tell that no good mama lie Tyrone Wang that I am hiding in the closet of this house when no one knows, and if I catch you one more time, I will whack his black ass with a baseball bat, you hear?"

The kid was gone in a flash, and Alex took some time to look at some of the faded pictures on the top of the fireplace, one showing a family of 12 people with a young mother holding a baby, marked, "Leyden 1938."

"Leyden, Leyden, I think that's a university town," Alex thought.

"Dear Lord, this baby must be the owner of the house. It says the baby was two years old, so now he must be about 35. I wonder what happened to the rest of the family."

Henny would not even entertain the question.

"Sometimes is better to let time heal things. Just a simple question may open old wounds and cause a lot of painful memories, so back off and stop dwelling in the past."

"Let people be."

Upon further investigation, it turned out that there was a whole row of apartments where the synagogue had placed aging Holocaust survivors, one of whom knew the story of the man from Leyden.

"He is the only one left out of extended family of 17," she said.

"All of them perished in the Holocaust. He is the baby in the picture."

For Alex, the circle had closed. He met the perpetrators of this outrage back in Austria. Now, thousands of miles away, he had faced the victims or their children. The only question was, "Why, why in the world would anyone commit such a senseless crime? Why?"

Henny had an explanation.

"Europe is a curse. These people have been killing each other for twenty centuries or even more, so there is no way out of the circle of violence. God bless America, and may God bless the day we came here."

After this unpleasant incident, Alex returned to his regular duties just to get a service call at an address a few streets away from Henny's shop. When he knocked on the door, an older black lady let him in the living room where she introduced him to her grandson, his friend Rodney Brown.

"Very nice to meet you Rodney, how is your school going?" Rodney's face was whiter than the wall. He tried to say something, gesturing behind his grandma's back: "Please don't tell my grandma about the brick, she'll kill me, she'll surely kill me."

The next day, as Alex came back from a service call, he heard the sound of a transistor radio playing Marvin Gaye's "How sweet it is to be loved by you" and saw three girls in red, green and yellow miniskirts, led by Rodney Brown himself, dancing in front of the store window as Henny, himself a fine dancer, looked on and snapped his fingers to the beat of the music. The song was so swell that Alex couldn't help but drop the toolbox and do a few quick steps himself, before the magic of the music was all but gone.

Rodney had something to say to him.

"Thank you for saving my life man, thank you for keeping my grandma out of this. I don't want to break her beautiful heart and make her cry. She is the only thing I have."

"You want to get a hamburger, kid? My treat," Alex said.

"Sure sir, I'd appreciate it."

As they walked across the street to Sally's Diner, Rodney started telling Alex how his father was arrested by the Detroit police for possession of cocaine with the intention to sell, and then ended up in jail. He had lost his mother due to drug overdose, and then the only place he could go was his grandma's.

"There is a girl across street named Ayesha. I will marry her when she grows up, and we will have a family."

As they sat in the diner, Henny's driver Howie Short and shop's chief technician Dom Pascuale, who Alex introduced as Dr. and Mrs. Sillyvan, joined them.

The two were trying to impress the young man by moving their thumbs up and down with eyes almost closed, claiming American women are like " | " and Asian like "--," as Rodney was listening in complete disbelief.

"Those two cats are the silliest SOBs I ever seen in my life. No wonder you call them the Sillyvan's."

The kid appeared to be bright and sincere yet was locked in a circle of bad friends that were for sure to con him into committing some crime.

So after this day, Rodney came often to the store and talked to Alex about almost everything, starting from electricity to the old Greek alphabet, from Dr. Martin Luther King to the stock market to Longfellow. He appeared to have a phenomenal memory and was absorbing information like a sponge. Rodney had a beautiful voice, and after he was taught the basic scales of music and how to read them, he would go to the library, get music sheets, and learn how to sing them on his own.

Alex was astonished.

"This kid has the brightest future one can imagine. I have never seen such a brilliant young man. Perhaps he will become an attorney or even the President of the United States."

"I wouldn't go that far, but if he manages to get his high school diploma without getting in any trouble with the police, he'll definitely be ahead of his peers," Henny said.

"I personally know hundreds of people as brainy as he is who still ended up in jail for years."

"You are a cynical old man Sol, a cynical old man," Alex countered.

"I have been watching this street for over 50 years, and I have very few illusions about what people can do to themselves."

So the friendship between the two continued for almost a year, during which Rodney learned how to read the stock tables of the "Wall Street Journal" and the "Barron's" magazine and even how to speak some rudimentary Latin phrases.

Then one day Rodney vanished. After not hearing from him for almost two weeks, Alex passed by the house just to find it empty.

"His grandma passed away, and he went back to Detroit to stay with his father who just got out of jail," Ayesha said.

"I will miss him so much. He was my best friend."

"Perhaps its better for him," Alex thought.

"Maybe he will graduate from high school and even make it to the university. I think he has very bright future."

"Amen," Henny said.

"Lord hears our prayer."

During his stay with Henny Alex had amassed in his bank account $5,375.66. He and his brother Ted scouted the Northeast part of town for a possible business location of their own, since both of their current jobs were very far from home. The location they were looking for turned out to be the Martin's building on Maple Square, a main street area that divided the very segregated black and white community in town.

Henny was not impressed.

"You will fail. You don't have the capital or the experience to survive in a private business. At any rate, you can always come back. I like your work ethics and character."

Chapter 5

Maple Square Electronics

So far, the first two years of Alex's life in the United States had been a roller coaster ride of social circles. Now in the new business, he and his brother met a new group of customers, the Appalachians, mostly white people from Kentucky and West Virginia (i.e., the hillbillies), some very uneducated and impoverished.

The mountain people of Appalachia were even more original characters than the blacks, starting with their language, music and customs. Every Friday, Ray Richards music store next door will have a bluegrass band led by the fiddle player Mr. Jim Ledu cover the latest country hits, followed by a comic presentation of a young woman doing back speak (speaking English backwards when stopped by a cop), and some square dancing by a group called the Moonshines.

Alex could not believe how much the bluegrass sounded like the folk music of the British Isles and was impressed to hear the lead guitar player of the band perform the famed Beethoven piece "Fur Elise" backwards.

These people may have struggled without much money, but talent and originality was abound and very visible.

There was a dark side of the Appalachians, naturally. Every day around ten, the Haggard cousins will slowly pass by the store window on the way to Ronny's Bar to get their first drink of the day, showing the longest middle finger in the universe, followed by a nasty missing-front-tooth grin adorning the yellowest teeth one can imagine.

Keith Cartwright, the building custodian, did not like them, calling them the Laggard's twins, and had to go with a baseball bat in hand to collect the rent and in many cases to restore order once a drunken squabble had broken out again.

It was not unusual to see vicious fights break out behind the store where scores were settled. One morning the brothers witnessed two men punching each other and rolling in the blood-covered snow until the police arrived and took them away.

Every day, a brown window van adorned "The Ministry of Heavenly Salvation" would make a couple turns around the square, and once they were sure there are no cops around, it would graciously park in front of George the Lebanese's store, letting out Bradford Greaves, a spectacular gentleman with a green feather in his hat and a few of his women.

Reverend Greaves, a convicted felon, had discovered God during his stay in the San Quentin State Prison and used the abundance of time courtesy of the good people of California to study and get his Doctorate in Theology from a respected university down south, after which he founded "The Ministry of Heavenly Salvation", geared towards homeless and abused, mostly white teens.

He picked up homeless kids from the street, provided them with shelter and food for a few months and then asked them to leave or provide money to help the Ministry, since the space in the dorm was very limited and food expenses astronomical.

Some would leave, but a lot of young women liked his fatherly appearance and started working for him, meeting some customers provided by the bouncer of Ronny's Bar, a man known as Mr. Mo Go Haynes, for half-hour rendezvous at random times upstairs in the Martin Building to avoid a raid by the Vice Squad.

Some of the dirt bags wouldn't pay, and it was not unusual to see through the window of the bar Mr. Mo Go holding a two-inch blade under the chin of some character, impressing upon him the virtues of the Ten Commandments in a show of force designed to remind all present that anyone who was messing up with Reverend Greaves' girls apparently hadn't heard of a place called San Quentin.

With the daily element of danger, many desperate people on the edge and ready to explode in rage, the brothers had to tread water carefully with the many criminal types in the area.

Despite the almost daily fights around the building, Alex was amazed by the persistence of the Appalachian people in viewing Ronny's Bar as a place of worship and social interaction. In fact, it was not unusual to see a family with three or four kids park their car in front and then have lunch, ordering five or six miniature hamburgers for the same price one could get a whole bucket of chicken just across the street. But this was a place where a lot of black people would have lunch in Church's Fried Chicken, so the whites preferred Ronny's mini burgers rather than getting mixed up with people of color.

America was still a very racially segregated country, a term that the brothers did not understand very well at the time.

The violence of the street was a daily occurrence of completely unpredictable magnitude.

A pipe bomb exploded into the gaming

parlor three doors down. The word on the street was that since the proprietor had not leased the machines from the local mafia Don, more of the same was to be expected unless they gave him a call.

Many years later on her deathbed, Mother Mary said that a friend from West Virginia had confided that her husband and two sons were killers for hire, hitting people all over the Midwest, then taking the bodies to the family farm for burial. The American streets were certainly places one had to be careful of friendships and associations.

To start the business, the two brothers would drive around on trash pick-up day with the blue Dodge van and pick-up refrigerators, TVs and radios left on the curb or buy used electronics from the newspaper. All the equipment was then cleaned, fixed, and resold to low-income customers for a reasonable price. Soon the African Americans discovered the store, and all of a sudden things became busy, with the stream of customers broadening to include some with jobs in major corporations. As newcomers to America, both brothers always thought that the sidewalks of America were lined with gold and in time, everyone could have a piece of gold of his own. They found very soon that not only there were no golden sidewalks, but also in certain places, there were no sidewalks at all.

There was a senior African-American gentleman, 25-year Army veteran Mr. Gill Williams, who recently started bringing his business to the store. Gill had spent years in Germany and Korea and clearly understood the terrible dangers the family must have gone through to make it to freedom and gain political asylum in the US. Not surprisingly, a very cordial and friendly relationship developed, and soon he'd drop in almost every day just to take a break from caring for his two grandchildren after a recent heart surgery. He would leave an old, almost blind man called Don Brady to take care of them for few hours.

One day, Gill called early in the morning complaining that his TV set had lost the picture and asked if someone can stop by and see if it could be fixed without visiting the store.

Alex jumped in the blue Dodge van and in no time was down below the bridge on Hickory Street in the heart of the ghetto, where scores of shantytown houses on sticks were scattered in yards covered with wild vegetation, abandoned cars and other junk.

When he finally found 347 Hickory Street, Alex could not believe his eyes. An older gentleman with completely white hair and a beard, clearly Don Brady, was sitting on the porch and two boys, in their underwear and absolutely filthy, were right next to him. Gill had driven himself to the hospital because of severe chest pains.

Alex entered the house to check the TV and immediately noticed there were rats running around, the kitchen sink was full with dirty dishes, there was no hot water, and the only working thing in the house was the telephone. An attempt to start the hot water failed when it turned out that the water heater valve was leaking.

Something had to be done to start the hot water, give the children a bath and perhaps run the critters out of the house.

Calvin Kelly who was working for the Health Department as a facilities inspector offered his assistance, showing up with two white guys in special protection gear ready to lead the effort to get rid of the rats. Ted brought his propane torch. With the hot water running again, a long hose was used to give the two boys, 8-year-old Billy Jr., and 5-year-old Kenny, their first shower in months as a river of dirty black water poured over the porch.

All clothes, bed sheets and dishes were also washed, and a large hole burrowed in by the critters as their house entry was filled in, the house apparently sitting on a whole colony of rats. Kelly and his professionals filled up all the entry holes with large, candy-like cubes designed to kill them but safe for children to play around.

When everything was said and done and everyone was dressed in clean clothes, it became obvious that the grandchildren of Williams were two spectacularly good-looking young men. So was Brady, after Kelly gave him a porch haircut and beard trim. On the way out and with Brady's permission, some of the junk littering the yard was also picked up and trash bins dragged to the street.

Before he left, Kelly was philosophical: "Do some good and the children will remember you, always remember you."

Remember they did, when after about 15 years during the Reagan Revolution, Alex and Kelly were driving toward a bankruptcy auction and got pulled over by a tall, slender motorcycle cop even though Alex was driving well below the speed limit. The cop checked the papers in a polite way, yet there was a strange grin on his face until Kelly saw his nametag: "B. Williams. "

"Ain't you the grandson of our friend Mr. Gill Williams, Officer?"

Yes he was, and the two got out of the car. Five feet six inches Kelly could not believe how tall

Billy Williams was.

"I think we ought to cut this man and his motorcycle in half so the state of Ohio will gain one extra cop and save on taxes," he proposed.

"Or perhaps we need to strip him naked and hose him off again, this time with cold water."

Now the motorcycle cop was in trouble, caught in between two angry uncles.

"Listen guys, I am very sorry to stop you, but I just wanted to say "thank you" for your kindness when my grandpa was ill."

Apparently Williams had passed away, and so had Brady, but the mother was back after serving her sentence for drug possession. Kenny was having a stint with the Navy.

"I told you the children remember, they always do," Kelly said as the two resumed their trip to the auction.

"May the Lord bless all of us and may He remember our friends Williams and Brady," Alex prayed, his voice breaking in emotion.

"You are sounding more and more like a preacher."

"Amen," Alex concluded.

This was the first time someone has said "thank you" to him for helping people.

As the range of customers seeking service grew around the city, the two brothers started visiting the familiar neighborhoods where Henny and Mr. Panser have been roaming for years and in fact getting into areas with a lot of gang activity and drug dealings.

One day Alex was called to a debilitated two-story building in the eastern part of the city and the moment he entered the front door, he knew there was trouble brewing on the horizon. The customer turned out to be a young black prostitute with her robe torn all over and her legs and other parts plainly visible. The john was a black man snoring in the bed with a mountain of cigarette butts and a half-empty bottle of whiskey prominently displayed on the night table.

Alex was as uncomfortable as one could possibly be and repaired the TV in few minutes, handing the bill to the girl and ready to fly away when she started talking.

"Do you remember me Sir? I is Ayesha, the friend of Rodney Brown, long time no see you honey. I work now for Rodney, he is my pimp, and he is rich, very rich."

If the roof of the building had fallen off, Alex could not have been more surprised. The kid that learned to speak Latin, play music, use trigonometry and could recite Longfellow, yes that kid Rodney Brown has become a pimp and a drug dealer.

Henny was of course correct again, the boy took the criminal path of his hoodlum father instead of using his enormous intellect and talents to go the right way and make himself a force of good in the society.

"Please give him my best regards, I am glad he is doing well," Alex muttered breathlessly.

"Oh, I definitely will. He constantly talks about you and would like to see you again."

Alex ran down the dirty stairs and out of the building, just to find a crowd of ugly and hostile black men surrounding the blue Dodge van.

"Where you going motherfucker? We heard you talking to the boss woman."

"Such a tragic end to a life full of promise and dreams, I cannot believe the end came so suddenly and so brutal. If there is God, he better appear to me very soon, please Lord, very soon," Alex prayed.

The prayer must have been heard if not by God, then by someone very close to him, because a cream-colored Cadillac pulled over suddenly and a very, very familiar voice chanted, "Hey guys, lay off, would you? Step aside. This is my main man Alex, my friend Alex."

"Thank you Lord, thank you very much, Sir," Alex whispered, looking at the sky.

God had incarnated himself as a quite tall and very good-looking black man Rodney Brown, flanked by two women, one blond and one brunette.

Little skinny Rodney had grown to be over six feet tall and very handsome, admired by women, and judging by the response of the rowdy crowd, probably more feared than respected. After giving Alex a big hug, he grabbed him by the shoulders and looked straight into his eyes, exclaiming, "It so good to see you again teacher, so good to see you. I have been telling people about what you taught me as a child, all these wonderful things about the world."

"I see that you are applying some of the things we learned about business in your private corporation already," Alex suggested.

"Quite a crowd is watching the store. Almost got me into big trouble for talking to Ayesha upstairs."

"I am very sorry about that my man, and I apologize and we apologize, ain't we guys? Listen, I'd like you to come to my house, remember the house where you caught me with the brick, and you meet my uncle Tyrone Wang, next Friday at 8 PM, you hear?"

As he drove away and finally got his heartbeat under control, Alex was already wondering what Kelly, with his doctorate in inner city matters had to say about all this.

"Damned if you go, damned if you don't. If you don't, they will come to Maple Square and start trouble for you and your brother. If you go, you may get caught in one of those gang shootings and find yourself early on page 2B obituaries or simply get beat up by some punks. At any rate, I rather be me than you."

It was to be a quite a long week until next Friday when Alex went back to the house through the bodyguards and found himself back in front of the very familiar fireplace where that fateful encounter had taken place a decade or so ago. It turned out that Rodney had two children with his mistress, living in a house adorned with a Steinway baby grand piano, the whole collection of Longfellow's books on the shelf and a box with the latest issues of the "Wall Street Journal."

"I want these kids to learn the things you showed me and to get a better life than me. And now I got the best surprise for you my man, I want you to meet my uncle Tyrone Wang. You remember him, don't you?"

Alex was glad that he had met Rodney and not Wang with a brick in his hand since Tyrone appeared to be almost seven feet tall, seem to weight 300-plus pounds, and had a face you wouldn't want to encounter in a dark alley.

"Rodney was telling me you wanted to whack my ass with the baseball bat, didn't yaw?" he said jokingly.

"Just a figure of speech, trying to steer the

kid out of trouble, horsing around with him," Alex replied.

"To take care of you, I need a telephone pole, not a baseball bat."

Tyrone was touched by the remark.

"By the way, thank you for caring about him during that time. It helped him a lot."

On the way out, Rodney turned to Alex and finally asked the question that was on his mind.

"What you think teacher, I did fine, didn't I? Please tell me the truth, even if it may hurt."

"Listen Rod, you have two beautiful kids and a lot of money. Sell everything and get out of town while you still can. Save yourself now."

"Thank you for telling me man, thank you very much, I'll surely consider it."

Kelly was unimpressed by the story; "You can't run from these motherfuckers even if you run to the end of the world. The cartels will find you, dead or alive."

A year had passed since this conversation took place when Alex read a police report that a drug dealer involved in prostitution had been gunned down in the western part of town by a rival gang. Kelly brought in the bad news.

"It was him, led into a trap when Ayesha started working supposedly for another pimp. He followed her, killed her, and then was gunned down by the other gang henchmen".

It was a sad and tragic end to another senseless loss of life in the ghetto, another two children without a father, another life wasted in crime instead of talents and gifts spent in search of a better life and service to family and community.

During the spring of 1973, Alex miraculously passed the entrance exam of the

University of Akron College of Sciences, Department of Physics to be exact, even though his English skills left much to be desired. Fortunately, he was assigned to the class of one very kind and caring teacher, Dr. Marta Goldstein, who was absolutely horrified to hear his English language structures, in violation of all grammar rules and accepted norms of civilized society.

"Alex, you speak English like a barbarian, and I will take the caveman hide of your back and turn you into a distinguished American intellectual," she would say softly.

So after a couple years in her classes and reading books from Early American Literature to the writings of Lincoln up to the modern masters, Alex started to laugh when Americans laughed and cried when Americans cried, he had in fact started his transformation of becoming a true American. At the same time, the family was watching with weary eyes the raging Vietnam War and ever-expanding Watergate crisis. Alex had volunteered to join the Air Force as a language specialist due to his training in Russian, German and Italian and willingness to study Chinese and Vietnamese. It was an open secret that there were Russian and Chinese advisers in Vietnam, so the military needed experienced ears to listen to all communications between the big boys and their Vietnamese cronies.

As Alex met some of the ROTC cadets in the university and had to make the very hard decision of which uniform to choose, the Air Force or the Marines, the eyes and ears of most people were glued to the TV and the daily proceeding of the Watergate commission that was deciding the fate of the country. Fortunately for all, the

American system passed the test and after a
peaceful transfer of power and presidential pardon
for Mr. Nixon, the Vietnam War ended in the
spring of 1975 and troops started coming back
home. Then came the bad news. Alex's academic
advisor Mr. Richard Hopkins informed him that
the application for admission to the officer corps
has been put on hold until he got his citizenship
papers, a date almost year and a half away. By then
he would have been 29 years old and above the
admissible age required to enter the officer school.
Clearly, it was not the destiny of Alex to become an
officer, and even though he accepted it in stride, for
many years after that he continued his support for
veterans organizations and was very proud to see
his son Simon become a Texas VA medical doctor.

The end of the Vietnam War was a
monumental event in the history of the country,
and a period of long and painful healing started.
On one hand, the hippie communes and the anti-
war movement started falling apart since their
greatest enemy was no longer around. On the other
hand, hundreds of thousands of war-weary veterans
started coming back home just to meet hostility,
ungracious countrymen, and the greatest enemy of
them all, the inability to heal the inner injuries and
visions of war terrors deeply ingrained in their
minds. Now that the war was over, the country had
to go back to normalcy after the 1974 stock market
crash had riled the markets due to Mr. Nixon's
resignation and war spending coming to an end.

Father Emo had suggested that Alex spend
more time studying the markets by subscribing to
the "Wall Street Journal." After all, the stock
market was the self-correcting mechanism that
allowed the American economy to keep investing

in the future and keep all enterprises most efficient and accountable to their shareholders. Though he was not enamored by the assignment, Alex started spending time in the university library reading the S&P stock sheets and charts because of his enormous respect for Father Emo. He was amazed by the complexity of the market theory and seemingly endless set of technical indicators the traders have developed over the years. Alex met a British graduate student named Dave Buckle, who was in the final stages of preparing his doctoral dissertation in Nuclear Chemistry and requested that he proofread the manuscript, help correct obvious mathematical, physics or logical errors that could sink his defense and infuriate his academic adviser.

Reading through the forty-some pages of equations, derivations and charts, Alex stumbled on a piece of paper where someone had noted a set of questions the examination committee might be inclined to ask, one in particular being, "Is your experiment Newtonian?" The question that immediately popped out in his mind was, "Is the Stock Market a Newtonian Experiment?" Dave had no idea, and neither did the academic advisor.

The best way to test the proposition was to then create a Newtonian relation and test it in the market, and if it led to some money, there must be something in the model that supported the hypothesis. Mr. Harlan Wineright, who himself has been investing in the market since the 1920s and not only survived the Great Depression but had been blessed to buy some 30,000 shares of the Goodrich Company for pennies on the dollar and now worth after all splits and dividends almost $15,000,000, offered encouragements and recommended wholeheartedly his broker at Bache Brothers as a good starting place for an inexperienced investor. The ball was now in Alex's court. He had to test his indicator on five components of Dow Jones Industrials Average to see if there is some correlation between the buy/sell signal and the subsequent movement of the stocks leading to a profit. The result was a disaster. After three months of testing, it became clear that the buy/sell signals had no relation at all on what happened on the next few days of trading. The indicator testing was abandoned, with Mr. Wineright suggesting that more time is spent watching the market decline and perhaps thinks of a new approach to the enigma that had captured the imagination of the young man. Alex started studying the early works of Einstein. They were incredibly difficult to read due to usage of tensor notation but still gave a clear path to understanding the underlying assumptions of the Theory of Relativity that had made him the most famous scientist since Sir Isaac Newton.

Alex deposited $7,600 in his account with Bache Brothers and was assigned to Mr. Wineright's broker Jeff Montand, one very sympathetic and charming young man who showed sincere support for the curiosity of his new client and did not spare effort to suggest investments that may be appropriate for him even in this rapidly declining market.

One Saturday in the summer of 1975, still thinking about his new project in the stock market on the way back from the university library, he remembered that Dr. Buckles had invited him to his going away party with lots of beautiful graduate students and candlelight music provided courtesy of the Ohio State University group of Ahmed and Palestinians, with a special appearance by Fatimah Hakish as Connie Francis. Since he never heard a version of "Where the Boys Are" in Arabic and not a single note of a Palestinian rock and roll ever, the temptation was too great to resist, so he decided to stop by, get a cold drink and perhaps have the once-in-a-lifetime opportunity of meeting the West Bank reincarnation of Elvis and Connie on the same day. After all, this was still a time the Middle East was perceived as a place of intrigue, magic, and romance, as depicted by the tales of "1,001 Nights," until a man called Youssef Arafat started throwing hand grenades at the West and turned the region into a nightmare.

Unfortunately, by the time he arrived, the Palestinian crooners and Fatimah were all gone. Everybody was dancing to the sounds of "Joy to the World," and drinks and drunks all around. Looking for a familiar face to talk to, he immediately noticed a girl in a red coat sitting on the couch, clearly uncomfortable and lonely. Always ready to help, he asked her for a dance, which she immediately declined. So instead of asking again, he sat next to her and started a funny and completely meaningless conversation just to make her look up at him and maybe start feeling little bit better. It turned out her name was Agnes, from the Philippine Islands and currently working on a Medical Technology internship in Ohio. People have said that a charming person is like a diamond covered with dry mud. You have to break the mud with your fingers before you see the shine. When Agnes pulled her hair on the side and looked at him, he saw two beautiful brown eyes, gorgeous lips and very delicate flat nose. She was so beautiful that he could not help but again ask her for a dance, to which she agreed if he taught her how to dance.

Agnes was educated by the holy nuns of St. Isabel, an all-girls school under the umbrella of the Jesuit Order and had very few social encounters in her young life, lacking basic modern skills like dancing, smoking or just hanging out with friends. Her first attempt at dancing was horrible, with her whole legs frozen like a little Teddy bear, but after couple of turns, she started to follow Alex and the music, so everything ended up with a smile.

Now he asked her for a date, which she immediately declined since he looked very suspicious and dangerous to her.

"Can I come and see you in your dorm?" he asked.

"Yes you can, but if you kiss me, you don't respect me, and I will have to use my hapkido skills to hurt you," Agnes replied after making a cat-like martial arts move with her hands.

Alex was deeply impressed and scared.

"I'd like very much to see you again, but at the same time, I don't want to find my smile three inches behind my left ear. Would you let me jump from the first-floor window before you strike that deadly hapkido blow, would you please Agnes?"

So on the first date, he went to her dormitory just to find a beautiful baby grand piano handy and no sign of Agnes. Being a patient man, he started playing some popular classics like "Moon River" and "Where the Boys Are" and then switched to some Chopin pieces. Soon, there was a small crowd of girl interns gathered around him, enjoying the music, but still no trace of the girl with the red coat.

"Have you seen Agnes around here, girls? I am supposed to have my first date with her and not with this piano, and I am about to start crying for her, really crying."

The joke changed everything since Agnes had been listening to the music all this time hidden behind the corner, and the girls were sent to check out Alex and report their observations later. So the first date ended up with laughter and a sigh of relief. After listening to the music of Alex for many weeks, the suspicions of Agnes seem to evaporate and she decided that despite his unconventional looks and ways, he was probably worth another look. After nearly a year of dating, the two were married in a nocturnal ceremony in the holy Mother of Mary Catholic Church, attended by hundreds of friends and family with flowers, songs, tears of joy, and flashes of cameras creating a river of emotion they never imagined.

Two years later they had their first child Simon, an incredibly charming little troublemaker, always curious to touch and dismantle everything. He was so small that Alex could put his head in the palm of his hand and his tiny legs next to his elbow. Simon had a soft spot on his head that terrified him, and when he was uncomfortable and crying, Alex would put on Agnes' nightgown in order to quiet him down and let him fall asleep. After six months of babysitting, full of love and amazement of the new life they had created, he started thinking that if all powerful men in the world were required to raise a baby of their own in their own hands, there could not possibly be another war ever. How could you send someone's son to die in a war after raising a child and trembling over it for years, living every day of his life as his own, celebrating every small victory, and putting a happy face on every small failure? It was a miracle, a miracle of new life.

Then came their second child Allan, a chubby boy with wavy brown hair, always ready to smile at a joke, with a healthy appetite for anything looking tasty, falling asleep only when his favored Linda Ronstadt music was being played. He appeared out of the blue like a miracle prince from the 1,001 nights story, completely different from his brother Simon, listening seriously to everything, including the stock market channel, the classical station WCLV and crying furiously if someone disturbed his peace in a rude way.

The family had bought their first house nestled under an enormous red maple tree, a house so old that one could see the ax marks on the floor beams. There was only half a basement surrounded by footer that soon was found to have a rat infestation. Calvin Kelly was glad to come in with his professionals and stuff the rat holes with the same candy-looking cubes used in Mr. Williams' house down on Hickory Street. The move suppressed the threat, at least for the time being. But there was another unpleasant surprise. Five-year-old Simon told Agnes he had a vision of an old red lady walking around, clearly an apparition since the neighbors reported seeing her for years and heard that someone died in a violent death in the house at the beginning of the century. Then the rats came back again. A friend gave the family one of her kittens with the hope that this would suppress the invasion. But then something happened that blew everybody's minds. Alex had come back from work just to find the cat on the walker of 1-year-old Allan, making a terrible

screaming sound, paw with claws fully extended
and ready to strike, right in front of his brown eyes.

The cat was kicked out for good and an
exterminator called again the next day. It was clear
the old hillbilly house was a curse, and the family
had to get out for the sake of the children, back to
grandma's house across the gorge. Pressed by his
unfortunate circumstance with the old house and in
need to build a new one to give the children a
better life, Alex was back to what Mr. Wineright
had called the problem of the century, that is how
to make some money in the market. After reading a
lot about relativity and metric tensors, he
composed a new indicator that seems to have a
better predictive record than the previous one. After
a few months of testing, it was time to jump in the
market ocean and see if one could catch some fish.
The GM stock had been followed for some time,
and one Wednesday, a definite "sell" signal was
given, meaning 400 shares of GM were shorted at
31.375 on the margin account Jeff Montand had
suggested as necessary for quick trading. Alex had
a sleepless night, blaming his reckless stupidity on
putting all the money they have saved with Agnes
on what could turn out to be a substantial loss
should GM start moving up again. Tired, with
bleary eyes and heart pounding wildly, he was in
Bache Brothers office right after the market
opening, immediately observing the mysterious
faces of Jeff and his partner Rich Paisley behind
the trading desk. This meant only one thing. He
had lost the bet and probably faced a margin call
since stock options were not yet invented. Alex
walked slowly toward the front of the trading desk
with legs so heavy that he could hardly move, and
then saw the ticker. GM was down 1 7/8 points,

and he had made some $581.36 after a hefty
commission (or 10 percent annual profit and his
salary for a month and a half) in one day of trading.

Father Emo and the family were in the
seventh sky, but the enthusiasm soon had to be
tempered by the realization that one spectacular
success was not necessarily the beginning of a
beautiful friendship unless the experiment could be
repeated flawlessly time and time again without
significant losses, as hedging was not possible
since the option market did not even exist. In
addition, affordable computing devices were not
available at all, and estimating the daily indicator
for few issues required significant time and power
with the usage of the university computer restricted
to assignments or graduate work.

This was the beginning of a lifelong
relationship as a market participant and student of
the free enterprise system, whereby Alex would
pick a trend and then ride it sometimes for years,
trading along for himself and the family, never
making millions but always making something
even in the worst circumstances. After all, the
market was the epitome of the supreme freedom in
which one does not need letter of recommendation,
state license or a diploma, just steel nerves and the
willingness to take risks.

His brother Ted, meanwhile, met a hippie
woman named Nancy, and was invited to visit her
home in the west of the city on a Sunday morning.
When all initial foreplay was said and done and the
time came to go to bed, it became plain that Nancy
was not really a woman but something in between.
Horrified, Ted grabbed his clothes, one foot in a
shoe, and jumped from the window in the back
yard, chased by the furious transgender person.

The good news was that he managed to throw his clothes over the fence and climb up in a flash. The bad news was that on the other side, Ted immediately recognized he was in the backyard of Henny's synagogue, where some hundred or so Orthodox Jews, in their black clothes and cherry-red Vermont canes in hand, were scrolling the compound, sharing the joy of the Sabbath with their families and friends. Seeing a young, almost naked man offending the sanctity of their temple infuriated the crowd beyond belief.

"Imbecile, pervert!" they shouted as Ted ran through a shower of angry canes that hit him all over. Fortunately, the terror lasted only seconds and life saved, when Rabbi Schulman who by Divine Providence happened to be in the yard with Henny, screamed, "Stop! That's enough, let him go."

"You are breaking the Ten Commandments on the Sabbath, aren't you, friend Ted?" the Rabbi mysteriously whispered.

In severe pain and almost out of breath, he tried to say something, but words were absent as he finally managed to put his clothes back on.

"You go in peace now, and think about the Sabbath whenever you can," the Rabbi said softly as Ted was on the way out.

Henny was deeply impressed.

"If I may make a confession in the winter of my life Rabbi, in my youth I was not as fortunate as this young man. May I proceed?"

"Some secrets are best kept forever, kept between you and God and away from your wife," the Rabbi said with an enigmatic smile.

"Especially from your wife. Let it be."

As for Ted, the lesson was very clear: Stay

away from progressives, and stick to basics. To this
end he got together with a woman from the old
country named Mirna, whose relatives had been
Eastern Orthodox priests since the time the
Apostles had landed in Greek Macedonia and
whose face looked like the icon of Holly Mother
Mary adoring the wall of her father's church. They
raised a beautiful daughter Lisa, and lived happily
until 2008 when Myrna lost her battle with cancer.
By the late 1970s, the brothers had received an offer
from Mr. Harlan Wineright, who as director of
many local corporations had invited them to join a
company named Metal Structures Incorporated as
machinist-programmers. It was a tempting
proposition and the job paid well, giving the
brothers the opportunity to get out of the old rat-
infested houses and move to better and healthier
neighborhoods. So they sold the business to a
partnership of Kelly and Reverend Smith,
remaining as advisers for another two years.

Chapter 6

The Reagan Revolution

The new corporate job put the brothers in an all-white environment they had never seen before and under the supervision of Plant "Commandant" Seth Glazer. Seth was a tall man with big green eyes and a thick Southern accent, born and raised in Memphis in a traditional Republican family who did not hide his dislike of newly arrived foreigners. His people came from middle Germany at the beginning of the century and despite having spent most of his life in the lively and cultured Tennessee, his natural Teutonic roughness gave the French saying, "love the people but not the Germans" a fresh new meaning. There was also a rumor that he may have been an official of a Southern Ohio Klan cell and there had never been a black person employed in his plant. No one knew why, but every morning Seth rode his motorcycle to the plant, showing up in the office dressed in suit and tie and boots covered in mud, like he'd walked through a pigsty. There was a warm greeting awaiting Alex on his first meeting with Glazer.

"I will be very fair with you. You can quit or I will fire you."

"Seth sounds just like Mr. Panser," Alex reported to Mr. Wineright.

"He's just trying to show his authority over you and has been known to do it to everyone in the plant. Don't let him make a habit of it. I will support you in any defense short of violence if this thing continues."

The company was staffed with over 100 paper white men, mostly first and second generation Americans and not a single black person on the payroll. This was shocking to Alex, who had spend the last eight years among mostly black people in the ghetto and deeply immersed in their ways and culture. The workers were proficient in their vocation, building large machining structures for the heavy industry, but aside from that, most had a pumped-up macho mentality of sports fanatics with their fancy football jerseys and the horrible notion that anyone with ambition for culture was a faggot, queer or at best a nerd. But the pay was too good to pass up, and the brothers decided to stay for a while and save money to hopefully move to better neighborhoods. With the vision of the cat paw in front of Allan's beautiful brown eyes and absolutely determined to get the family in a safe and clean house, a half acre of land on the top of the hill caught Alex's attention, a part of a homestead dating to the 1860s owned by an old lady Mary Penlan.

Due his education at the University of Akron, Alex tried to develop a plan to fend off the incoming surprises of Reaganomics, having been advised by the owner of the local numismatic store Mr. Richard Mulligan to purchase a portfolio of precious metals coins and build a large cash position in anticipation of the coming economic crash. But he found new friends that were about to have a profound influence on his life.

The eight members of the happy Paulino family were meeting the challenges of the coming Reagan Revolution as a well-balanced, highly diversified international corporation, whose business model was established by their

88

Portuguese grandfather and based on hard work, avoiding borrowing money at any cost or dealing with banks.

To this end, the family, including five-year-old grandson Tony, delivered up to 800 newspapers every morning, then after sleeping until noon, the men went to one of the local cemeteries and dug at least two graves per day with four custom-made shovels having the inscription, "Wherever you go, you'll be back here." The women on other hand baked Portuguese bread and pastries and tried to sell some at the local mall, thus helping to generate an incredible $4,500 a month after taxes, half of which according to Mother Paulino, was invested in silver and gold coins and half held in reserve.

Since the Paulino men were master diggers and according to the family legend had carved the grave of the great seafarer Vasco Da Gamma back in the old country, they dug their own Federal Reserve Bank no one knows where, deposited their riches in it, and always had someone guarding it with a shotgun that Father Paulino had bought on an estate sale for $25.

Fortunately, the expectation of Reaganomics had a positive side, having led to a pronounced rise in the price of gold and silver, thus increasing the value of precious metals holdings of Alex up to $12,000 and creating an opportunity to buy the lot of Mrs. Penlan as the site for his new house, provided he could convince the broker Mr. Packard to give it up for a lower price. But Mrs. Penlan was living in Coral Gables, Florida, unwilling to bargain and part with her lot.

Alex had recently met Mother Paulino in the local farmers market and could not believe his eyes to see her glowing like a light bulb when whispering, "Our gold investment is worth almost $100,000 now. Mr. Paulino can finally retire from digging graves and let the children handle the newspaper empire for themselves."

"You better cash in the gain now mom. These things go down the way they go up, before he gives up the grave digging franchise," Alex advised.

"I already sold my modest holdings and am ready to buy a half-acre lot up the road from here. The only thing left to do now is give Mr. Paulino a neat haircut, buy a pair of shiny leather shoes and join the Reagan Revolution."

"Amen Father," she whispered.

Finally there was a bit of good news as Mrs. Penlan, apparently unwilling to bother with her lot and in need of money, decided to sign on the dotted line and give it away for $12,000.

"You are a lucky dog, friend," Mr. Packard quipped.

"Aboard of a prestigious market and will surely make some money on the trade."

So Alex had parted with the gold and was finally an owner of a piece of Ohio land, land of an original 1865 homestead, right on the top of the hill with clouds floating just above the trees.

But his troubles with biased, irresponsible and rude Americans whom brother Ted had called "GEPs," for "Genetic European Peasants," were not over by any stretch of the imagination.

The neighbor was a man of Russian descent, a pattern maker in a furniture company down the road, who has changed his family name from "Ivan Nagornik" to more Saxon-sounding John Woodbar.

Mr. Woodbar was very clear: "We don't

want people like you in this neighborhood. You are not welcome here."

Alex politely explained the house was only for investment purposes, in fact he had been negotiating to lease it to a black gentleman with 14 children who liked to sing, dance and play basketball 24 hours a day.

"You are going to love this crowd. They will set the street on fire."

Mr. Woodbar was shocked by the news.

"You really want to let black people live in this house? Right next to mine? I cannot believe that."

"You'll be delighted to see 14 black faces every morning smiling at you. These guys are a lot of fun."

Mr. Ronny Williamson, the neighbor across the street, a highly decorated WWII veteran and a great American, was not amused when he heard the remarks of Mr. Woodbar.

"I always thought that Woodbar is an idiot. People like that give America a bad name."

At any rate, Alex never heard another hostile remark in the fourteen years the family lived there.

Securing a loan for a new house just before Mr. Reagan was sworn in office was to be much more difficult than expected. The loan officer had called Commandant Glazer's office and told that the contract will expire in March of 1981 with layoffs possible, Alex naturally right on the top of the list. Still, the bank was kind enough to grant an interview since the lot was paid in full and the couple had savings of almost $40,000 in cash or investments.

Expecting a definite rejection, Alex and

Agnes were very relieved to see Bank Director Mr. Melcher dwelling on a long list of profitable market trades in Canadian and South African mining issues instead of asking the haunted questions about Mr. Glazer's monstrous layoff plans and contract expiration. He was apparently a Canadian, raised and educated in Capetown where his father has been on the Board of Directors of many of the companies mentioned, sharing memories about South Africa and the difficulties the native people had under the Apartheid.

Mr. Melcher decision was quick and surprising.

"Someone having $40,000 in an environment of impending layoffs, demonstrated financial responsibility of having a paid lot and a history of successful trading is definitely the kind of person we like to extend credit to. I will recommend to the Loan Committee that your request is granted, and good luck with your new house," he warmly shook hands with Alex and Agnes before leaving.

An all-Amish crew worked long hours, and the house was up in six days, sweet smell of pine all around and white clouds floating right above the roof from behind the forest.

Down the hill from Alex's new house there was a patch of forest surrounding sleeves of water known as Silver Lake, where an old-timer named Mr. John Cunningham was living in an aged gray shack huddled among the trees. He was a jolly old fellow, very kind and always willing to discuss the world which he had traveled extensively as a sailor, so Alex and the children will pass every Saturday morning by the lake to have a chat with him, do some fishing or simply walk through the forest.

Like many old settlers, Mr. Cunningham was part American Indian from the Shoshone tribe and at night, as people gathered around the crackling yellow flames of the fire in front of the shack, he would start talking about the magic legends of the Natives and the spirit of every natural medium called Manitou.

"America has a very strong spirit," he would say.

"After few centuries, your face will become red and the Manitou of America will creep in you, rejoice you when she shines above, and offend and sadden you when she is put down."

"America is the kindest mother of them all I say".

Silver Lake was leftover from the magical forest that covered Ohio before the white man came, where you can see rose-eyed rabbits run through the bushes, flocks of green feather geese bathing with their ducklings in the marsh-covered water, and a family of deer will startle, jumping out of nowhere right next to you, then vanish like shadows in the dense brush. At night, Silver Lake was even more nocturnal, surrounded by majestic trees all around and brilliant stars above, one can see from the hill overlooking Mr. Cunningham's shack iridescent blue, orange and green lights dancing on gentle waves of the marsh-covered lake, like telling a story of times and people long gone.

When a man has happy days, they should try to enjoy every one of them to the fullest because they may never return, and this was true with Silver Lake. After coming back from a brief vacation, the family found a large bulldozer on the property, the shack of Mr. Cunningham leveled to the ground and large sign that read, "Silver Lake Apartments:

Early reservations welcome." The old man had passed away, with the body flown back to Idaho for a burial, so his niece sold the grounds to the developers even though his will postulated that the property was to be a wildlife preserve.

The scream of earth moving machines was on for months as parts of the lake were filled up, many trees cut down to make place for the new apartments, and even the hill overlooking the lake was terraced to allow extra space for the newcomers.

Gone were the ruby-eyed rabbits, the green-feathered geese had flown away, the deer moved up to the next forest, and soon the Silver Lake apartments were rented to some unpretty characters who wore thick glasses and drove mostly Japanese cars.

There was Nadim the Syrian, cited by the police for animal cruelty, trying to slaughter a sheep on the sidewalk in front of his apartment. Then there was the gay couple of Jay and Jess, and every morning at about 10, one could hear the sobbing of Jess, being given his daily spanking by his partner Jay, a part of gay ritual of life we are told. Further down the row there was the Chinese immigrant Zieng Wu, where one morning the immigration police arrested 21 illegals living in his two-bedroom apartment, and the list went on and on.

One of the most noteworthy and likable Silver Lake arrivals was the Korean War Veteran Mr. John Turnipcy, fresh to his new job as a truck driver in the local newspaper. Like most African-Americans, Mr. Turnipcy was a colorful person who did not spare words when the truth needed to be told and was still driving with great pride his

1967 Chevy Nova with all doors in different colors, a statement of defiance saying, "Black man ain't driving a Jap car." During the slavery, the family had been on a plantation down south, gathering as you may have guessed already, turnips. So the Master named the first family TurnipA, the second TurnipB and fortunately for him, his family was named TurnipC. Later on the slavery was abolished, the Civil Rights Movement under the leadership of Dr. Martin Luther King roared ahead, but Mr. Turnipcy was still stuck with his turnip past, so a convenient "y" was attached to his name to make his name a bit more likable.

Back in Commandant Glaser's factory, unfortunately for all workers with their fancy football jerseys, it was to become very clear that history is full with endless examples of people whose failure to read books, old newspapers and warning labels had been terribly detrimental and in fact fatal not only to themselves but to whole countries. Alex had recently read a dissertation related to an emerging science called "Chemometrics," an application of spatial statistics to description of environmental hot spots where persistent dumping of carcinogens and other toxins created danger to life.

So it did not take long to observe the fact that under orders by Commandant Glaser, the operators of the large machining centers and the paint shop workers were washing by hand every tool with a nauseous substance called chloratene, stored in three barrels in the middle of the main bay, one later on called "Cancer Alley," and right across from the main office. And that was not all. Almost empty barrels were taken to the back yard of the company and the leftovers dumped right next to the barbwire fence on the opposite side of which there was a row of brand new houses and some thirty yards to the right, a children's playground. Seeing blond Ohio babies playing around with loving moms watching them right next to a carcinogen hot spot gave Alex a sick feeling, so back to the barrels he was during the lunch break, reading the warning label clearly stating the cancer danger, the need to wear gloves, have respirators on and provide adequate ventilation when around the substance.

The peeled warning label did not impress Commandant Glazer. In fact, it made him mad.

"It ain't any of your business to tell your supervisor how to handle company's safety procedures. We have been using the stuff for years, and not until smart college ass like you mentioned, I ain't heard anyone complaining. Listen to me boy, and listen good or you'll be watching the front door from the outside."

With the visions of the blond babies in his mind, the first thing to do was to buy a pair of safety gloves for Ted, then report the matter to Mr. Wineright, who in turn reported it to the company president. It may have escaped Commandant Glaser's attention so far, but in late seventies and on, the state of Ohio and the Federal Government had launched an intensive campaign to clean the Ohio Valley to the tune of hefty fines and jail sentences intended to impress all polluters that dumping their trash in Ohio Rivers and soil will be punished mercilessly. But the pig headiness of the Commandant was so extreme and his irresponsibility so blatant that to expand on Cornelius Brown joke, if there were a coefficient of "orangutanity," the unit had to be 1G (1 Glazer).

Hence in two days, there was a visit by the brass, including the company president Mr. McHarden in his signature wheel chair pushed around by Mr. Wineright. Right to the wire fence they went, followed by a very gray Commandant Glazer.

All empty barrels were removed, the ground scraped down 6 inches and hauled away, gloves and respirators issued to all concerned, and strong ventilation introduced in the dangerous areas.

"I will deal with you later," Mr. Glazer whispered hatefully during the lunch break.

"They chew my ass down to the bone, and I am after yours, so watch your back, college boy."

"You are very welcome Sir, at least now the babies on the other side of the fence won't have to breathe your shit," Alex retorted.

So the barrel war was on with Commandant Glazer looking for every opportunity to get on his case or make him look bad in the eyes of the management.

Fortunately, he did not have to wait long for his revenge plans to come to fruition.

Unknown to the family, Father Emo had involved himself in the election effort of an obscure actor and currently the Governor of State of California named Ronald Reagan. They apparently met on the campaign trail somewhere and Mr. Reagan turned out to be a warm and nice fellow, who after hearing his story gave him a large poster of himself and Mrs. Reagan with the inscription, "To Emil with sincere admiration and friendship. Ron and Nancy."

It was prominently displayed on the wall of his office.

Mother Mary was furious.

"We ought to throw his suitcase out of the window and change the door locks right away. I don't want any Republicans in this house."

It was a great idea. Unfortunately, the house was in his name, and throwing an attorney out of his own house due to acute political differences was next to impossible. So the family shrugged the conflict in a truly American way and embraced his unwavering support for his favored politician.

Mr. Reagan's presidency started with a lot of fanfare and promises of tax cuts that were about to send the country on the road to new prosperity.

The trickling down of the fortunes of the wealthy to the ordinary Americans was to create a never-ending economic miracle based on personal responsibility and Divine intervention.

The experiment turned sour after only a few months as far as the brothers were concerned, when the company's prototypes of industrial welding robots were sent to our friends overseas, and many workers were laid off, part of a shock wave that had swept the whole country.

But brutality and suddenness of the economic collapse caught everyone by surprise, and the family had just moved out of the old, rat-infested house to the new house on the top of the hill.

Mr. Turnipsy was no fan of President Reagan.

"I ain't no Ain'tstein to know that Reagan is a hit man and kidney buster looking for tall, strong slaves to pick his cotton and turnips, you know what am saying? He ought to go abroad and get all the chinipcy rickshaws he wants. Black man ain't picking cotton and turnips no more."

Kelly was also reporting that the African American resistance and mistrust to the Republican onslaught was spreading as new music of anger called "rap" was sweeping the ghetto, and whole suburbs of Cleveland and Detroit were turning into war zones.

Mr. Ronny Williamson put it even more bluntly.

"This old Irish fart will paint himself in history as having started the destruction of the American industrial base, so in twenty years we won't even have bullets to defend ourselves. My friend Alex, we Americans are the dumbest asses in the world. We will sell grandma's false teeth for money."

It was shocking to see how many Americans were deeply disappointed that the bullet of the assassin Hinckley missed the target, saying, "The son of a bitch dodged the hangman, unfortunately."

As for Commandant Glazer, he was back to his old tricks and meaner than a junkyard dog, biting and scratching Alex at any opportunity, just waiting for the right reason to get rid of him.

There was no place to go but back to the wisdom of his newly found relatives, the African Americans. Anger started boiling in Mr. Turnipcy's big heart when he heard about the outrageous and rude behavior of Seth Glazer.

"We have been with this racist crap for over 300 years. In America today, you ain't nobody's God damn personal slave. My friend Alex, make sure there is nobody around, then tell the Klan motherfucker to let you be."

Alex was horrified.

"You sure he won't shoot me or burn a

99

cross in front of my house?"

"No he won't. These assholes are not as tough as you think."

Mr. Glazer was clearly stunned by the frontal attack, his eyes helplessly scanning Alex's face for any expression of fear, but there was none. Then he turned around and left. Alex did not hear another idiotic statement again and was later invited to Glazer's house for his birthday party, which he gracefully accepted.

The Reagan Revolution began slowly and boringly, but after a year or so, many companies started laying off large numbers of workers or completely closing their doors forever. Only the Paulino clan, with their firm rules of engagement, was weathering the crash without a blink of the eye. To see such a staunch cohesion in times when millions of Americans were unemployed and thousands of businesses were crushed by the supply side economics of Mr. Reagan was very refreshing and in fact highly educational for Alex and the family. Both Alex and Ted were laid off from Metal Structures Corporation and given 12 months of benefits due to the fact that they were both industrial workers. Having never been laid off before, it was very surprising to observe how many things around them became influenced by the sense of depression, worthlessness and rejection. A mutual friend, who had the audacity of making jokes even in the face of the worst crash since the Great Depression, introduced the brothers to a set of witticisms known as the McGregor Unemployment Theorem.

1. Layoff notice is to be received no later than a month after the senior vice president of the company had personally assured you that you are indispensable.
2. As soon as your last paycheck is exhausted, a major household expenditure will pop out.
3. Shortly after the initial estimate is received, it will be found that some dummy understated the amount by factor of two.

The Baumgartner observation also stated that, "The most annoying bills always show up on Saturday."

There was no need to seek proof of the theorem since only four days after the layoff, Alex put his Ford Galaxy gear selector into drive position and was shocked when the car moved only backwards. A quick call to the transmission shop produced a sense of relief with an estimate to adjust the clutches for only $125, but when the car was towed in the shop, the expense rose to $200, right in line with Mr. McGregor's predictions above. Mind over matter, as people have said on numerous occasions.

Every Monday, Alex will wrap his son Allan in a warm blanket and drive all over town to search for a job, then go to the unemployment office downtown to collect his weekly check since all job inquiries were always negative and North-Eastern Ohio business had ground to a halt. To make things even worse, there was long line of people waiting outside already, and since the size of the snow flakes and the rate of snowfall are directly proportional to the unemployment rate, the spring of 1981 was very cold and soggy, making the unemployment experience even more miserable.

In the process of being re-trained for a new vocation, both brothers were sent to an electro-mechanical school to acquire the skills necessary for repairing, installation and modification of industrial electric and electronic controls.

The facility was a place where large crowds of familiar unemployment office types would gather every evening, each with their own problems and horrifying story to tell.

There they observed a young, white, blond-haired woman named Janet, smoking cigarettes during the breaks and eating only one pack of potato chips per night. The husband had abandoned Janet and their two boys Cody and Danny after being laid-off, so she was keeping all food stamps to feed the kids, leaving herself hungry in the process.

Seeing a hungry person was something new and very shocking for the brothers, so they decided to each pitch in 50 cents and buy her a sandwich every night.

Being a proud American, she angrily refused, but since hunger is more primitive than pride, eventually accepted the offer with a great amount of gratitude.

After two months, Janet was referred to a repair job in Midland Automotive, so the brothers assumed conveniently that Mr. Reagan's trickle-down economics would take care of her and the kids, thus sending one less family to the unemployment office.

Eight long months had to pass before two openings for auto electrical repair in the local facility of the Meisner Motors were available, thus finally giving the brothers the opportunity to say "so long" to that unpleasant chapter of their lives, at least for the time being.

In the new workplace, Alex and Ted met two new friends that could not have been farther apart in their life story.

One was Adam Heyland, a blond Amish man who had left the family farm after getting tired of hauling horse manure to the fields and volunteered to the Air Force as a rocket specialist. Unfortunately, his application was rejected due his acute dyslexia, as the doctors decided that the missiles were more likely to land on his father's farm instead in Russia's Far East. His disappointment did not last very long since he met a long-legged, busty bank teller woman named Taylor James, who herself had run away to seek and experience the pagan delights of the outside world. It was a love at first glance for the enormous irritation and chagrin of the Amish elders back on the farm.

Life was all wine and roses for the lovebirds in the last months of the Carter Presidency, as Adam found an assistant manager's dream job in town's largest pet store. Checks were piling up so much that the lovebirds started to look for a nest to hatch some eggs into and raise ducklings of their own.

But then came the Reagan Revolution. The volume at the store drastically dried up, so in the spring of 1981, he was laid off with only six months of benefits to draw on.

The only place to go was the repair facility where he met the brothers and a crowd of desperate people, the most spectacular of which was of course Tim McHill, himself sidelined by the bankruptcy of a metal stamping plant in Cleveland.

Tim McHill was a well-built, dark-haired

Irishman with deep blue eyes and a look that had attracted women of all walks of life, including his greatest love Lana, a dogcatcher for the city of Twinsburg.

McHill spent two years on a navy ship patrolling the coast of Vietnam, frequently pounding Vietcong positions. On one of his shore leaves, he found himself in the middle of a firefight between Charlie and South Vietnamese Special Forces when an RPG explosion nearby sprayed him with hot shrapnel, causing severe injuries to his left arm and shoulder and sending him to the Hospital for almost two months. Tim was honorably discharged and arrived in San Diego in January 1973, arm still in a sling, just to be greeted by a crowd of hippie war protesters shouting, "Nixon traitors, murderers," and pelted with tomatoes and eggs that hurt his pride more than his injured body.

"I fought proudly for my country, I bled for it, just to arrive back home and be greeted by a bunch of paint snuffers hurling tomatoes and eggs at us. I have a score to settle with the hippies. I will show them you never throw an egg at an Irishman and get away with it."

So his private war never ended. Colonies of hippies were still intact, smoking pot endlessly and having sex orgies every night, giving him the idea to supply them with marijuana and get paid handsomely in the process.

He would buy the stuff from a black guy in Cleveland (who was also a Nam vet), in quantities of 50 pounds, and then partition it into bags of a half a pound, which in turn would be sold to his four suppliers in North-Eastern Ohio. A highly moral and religious man, he never sold a drop of pot to an ordinary American. He only sold to hippies, saying, "I want the sons of bitches to burn their asses with grass the way we burned ours in the rice patties of Nam."

The way he was choosing his buyers was absolutely brilliant. He would not even talk to a person until visiting the graves of all parents, and then drive to the library downtown to find the obituary's listing of family members, including the prospective contact. Once the connection was made, he would put a 1/2-pound bag in the middle of a bouquet of flowers and leave it at the grave of the deceased at a completely random time, not forgetting to make the sign of the cross before leaving. The buyer then must pass by Tim's job, find the old Ford truck, and toss the envelope with the money in a barrel of quarters that was securely strapped to the bed. Failure to pay was not an option since he already knew the whole family and was also carrying a large caliber shotgun to underscore the point.

The proceeds from the pot trade had allowed him to buy two double wide trailers near Lake Milton, one for his aging mom and one for himself and hopefully the dogcatcher woman one of those days.

So he traveled every Monday down to Canton with the pot buried a foot underneath the quarters, then would return to Youngstown on Friday and spend a wild weekend with Lana.

Tim was working only part time and living in the old Ford with all the paper currency stowed below the bed in a specially built inconspicuous "safe" able to hold about $10,000 at any given time. Since it was very strange for people to see someone regularly under his truck for no reason at all, he would lay down below and bang his gas tank a couple of times, as to determine the amount of fuel by the dullness of the sound coming back at him and of course put or retrieve money from the "McHill Bank" as he proudly liked to say. Shrewd those Irishmen, very shrewd, Alex thought many times.

But the Irish luck was a tricky woman as McHill was about to find out the hard way.

On one rainy Friday the 13th, McHill was carefully guiding the old truck on the way back to Youngstown after a very successful week that had netted him almost $5,800. Unknown to him, he was being trailed by a car of two elevator repairmen who had just decided to split a large deluxe pizza as they were trying to stay in line on the slippery road in a silent drizzle and sudden gusts of wind.

Then trouble hit. A family of deer crossed the road, and as he slammed the brakes to avoid hitting them, the truck got rear ended by the elevator repairmen, who did not even have time to drop the pizza on the floor.

The old Ford could not handle the enormous stress of the collision. The bed caved in, and the bottom of the barrel which turned to be very rusted from the Ohio salt, sheared off and started spilling his treasure on the road, leaving a streak of coins forty feet long.

McHill was furious, but not for long since an OHP sergeant was at the site of the accident almost in a flash and his $5800 still in the safe under the bed.

He produced a careful ¾ smile as the elevator people were found to be at fault, but then trouble started again. The officer wanted to ticket him for not properly attaching the barrel with quarters to the bed, thus endangering public safety, with the amount of the fine considerably greater than all the treasure lying on the side of the road.

Then the Irish luck shined again. The sergeant noticed the old Navy shirt he always wore, and miracle of miracles, it turned out his son was Tim's shipmate in Nam and in fact was present during the shameful attack on the streets of San Diego in the winter of 1973.

So the ticket book was put back in the patrol car, and instead broomstick and dustpan kindly provided as McHill and his brother-in-law labored for almost two hours to collect every quarter they could dig out of the mud on the side of the road. It was a very close call with a happy ending, but as he liked to say, troubles come in streaks.

Shortly after this fateful accident, the Meisner Motors, the owner of the facility, filed for Chapter 11 bankruptcy, leaving some 130 workers back on the street again.

Adam had no place to go but back to the Amish Farm and the horse manure as the brothers started their own newspaper empires following the example of the Paulino family.

McHill's troubles were far from over.

His dear mom, who had been fighting emphysema for years, finally succumbed to the illness and passed away in the winter of 1991. Heartbroken, he decided to sell the two double-sided trailers and head out West since all hippies were already moving there. But then an even more terrible blow followed. Ignoring the old rule that a crook never tell all his secrets, especially to the woman he loves, he had divulged to the dogcatcher woman that some of his money was hidden in a container buried below one of the trailers. No one knew for sure, but there was a suspicion that the future father in law, who himself was facing a ruin due to a mortgage default, was the one who cleaned him out of $37,500. So the dogcatcher love was gone and a heap of money up in smoke.

"Easy come, easy go," as people would say. With $65,000 left from the pot trade and in a very nice, low mileage S10 truck, he took to the West, leaving all his troubles behind, finding himself in Beverly Hills in four days.

A charmer of women, McHill apparently found a job taking care of the dogs of a famous actress. It lasted only ten days. He was back on the street again, after the dogs made a poopoo on the shoes of the husband, according to the postcard sent back to Ohio.

Ambitious and determined, he applied for a job on the biggest golf club in the city but was rejected right away, showing up to the interview unshaved and untidy, having slept in the S10 on the side of the road. Undeterred, he applied again, this time looking his best, just to meet the Club Manager, who not surprisingly was a Navy vet, and had him hired to drive the carts with VIP visitors around the property.

Then the postcards stopped, and no one heard of him for years.

Meanwhile in Ohio, it seemed that the men with the blue suits were trying to convince the men in the blue jeans that everything was all right as the green pastures of the bright Republican future were getting distant by the day and more unemployment and bankruptcies were spreading across the country.

But the truth is like a septic tank as the

smell eventually would creep out, and there was no way to hide.

Alex had stumbled on Commandant Glazer and the Tennessee woman in a store near their home and was absolutely shocked to see the usually cocky and sure Seth, bursting with strength and excellent health, to be a dark shadow of himself, eyes sunk in his pale face, skin and bones, and looking tired and sickly. The 45-year-old company had gone bankrupt and sold for pennies on the dollar with all 146 workers laid off and pensions lost completely.

He had been diagnosed with terminal lung cancer and given no more than six months to live, the first of five people on Cancer Alley that had contracted the disease, as we shall find later on.

Alex was heartbroken to see the big green eyes of the Tennessee woman full with tears, gave Seth a hug and watched them slowly walk away.

But troubles keep coming in streaks as the very wise Tim McHill had observed, just piling up and worse by the day.

This became painfully clear the next day when someone wildly started ringing the bell of the house. When he opened the door, Alex was surprised to see the Appalachian girl Janet at his doorsteps.

"Sir, please take me to West Virginia, please," she pleaded breathlessly, her eyes full with tears.

"Janet please come in, are you alone? Where are the boys? How did you find me?"

"Please Sir, take me to West Virginia."

Her face was pale and aged, her beautiful blue eyes cold and distant, her blond hair in shambles. She was not making any sense and repeating the same phrase endlessly.

So he had to drive her all the way to the Ohio turnpike truck stop, where they found a very nice mom and dad couple driving their own rig just about to take off east toward Pennsylvania.

The mom was almost in tears when she heard Janet's story, and after giving her a hug, said, "Our own daughter went through horrible unemployment and divorce recently. Don't worry honey, mom and dad will take you home, don't you worry."

All Alex had on himself was $27 to spare and then waved at her, watching the rig slowly crawl in the turnpike lane heading east.

It was not clear at all what had happened to the two boys Cody and Danny, so the next day Alex met with Janet's former supervisor Hank Cheadle. The news was not good. The husband, still hopelessly unemployed and depressed, had taken the boys out for a treat, then drunk and on drugs headed on the way down to West Virginia.

There was an accident and he was surely killed, but Hank heard that the boys were hurt but still alive.

Then another cluster of troubles hit two weeks later as Ted's right hand collapsed just above the wrist, and to the shock of the family, bone cancer was the reason. His life was expected to end within two months.

Alex never been in a cancer ward, and to see row after row of terminal patients, the majority of whom had lost jobs, family and businesses due to the sharp contraction of the Reagan Revolution was difficult to handle even for a person who had crossed the minefields of the Iron Curtain and had witnessed the terror of the KGB.

Next to Ted there was a young black man called Harvey, a former mainframe computer salesman who had contracted terminal colon cancer after losing his job and house. Across the hall, there was a white woman dying from breast cancer after she and the husband had lost their meat processing plant and home due to bankruptcy.

So what can a man do sitting between two dying young men, counting the days left and unable to think what to say that will make any sense or give any hope at all?

Alex would push them to the MRI tube, watching with silent suspense the number of bright dots showing the spread of the cancer. Ted had twenty-eight, and Harvey had twenty-one.

Then he started praying even though he never read the Bible in his life.

Back in the old country, Alex had been through what in America is called a near-death experience on his birthday on December 21, 1968.

He substituted for a friend of his, a teacher in a small village in the mountains above his hometown of Varna. Not surprisingly, his East German Trabant car was frozen solid, and he had to take the bus on the way back, walking a mile through the frozen and windswept field. About a hundred feet from the bus shelter on the main road, he felt of being not alone and when he looked around, saw a wolf pack silently closing on him from three sides, hopping through the deep snow. Alex ran for dear life and once on top of the bus shelter tied his hands to the corner of the roof with his shoe laces, a circle of eyes around and hungry wolves jumping high, trying to take him down.

It was around 6 PM already, and a

snowstorm was blowing hard. He knew he was about to die soon, but at least he wouldn't be torn to pieces by the wolves. Many hours had passed and almost unconscious, he heard gunshots as hardly opened his snow-covered eyes to see a truck and three men chasing the wolves away.

There was no room in the cab, so he was put in the back and covered with tarp during the trip back to his house in the city.

He remembered that the door opened, his friends shouted, "Happy birthday," and then he fell unconscious into the hands of Ted.

What happened after was even stranger. He was on his back, floating in a shower of blue stars, absolute peace and bright light, light of living gold above.

At the same time, he could see himself below in an emergency room with a young doctor and a nurse attending to him.

Alex had been in a coma for four days, when he finally came back and opened his eyes to see Mother Mary and Father Emo next to him.

Several days later while walking home, he met a well-dressed young man and his beautiful wife crossing the street next to his house.

"I am very sorry to bother you, Sir Doctor, but I like to thank you for taking care of me in the hospital. Thank you very much, really."

The man's eyes were in absolute amazement.

"How do know me? You were in a coma for days. This is impossible."

A few days later, in the apartment with Father Emo and entering one of rooms, Alex noticed a bright light just above the ground. It was Christ, surrounded with living gold, looking at them.

"Father, look, Christ is there, in the corner," he exclaimed, pointing toward the wall. Father Emo could not see him.

Christ had long black hair, a narrow, very strong white face, scant beard and eyes, eyes so horrible that they were literally pushing you to the floor on your knees. He was angry, very angry, and wanted them on their knees, as one should be in the presence of God, which Alex did for the complete amazement of Father Emo.

Mother Mary reported the vision to the church, and everyone started to make the sign of the cross, after all, seeing Christ is always harbinger of good.

So Alex would sit between Ted and Harvey, hold their hands, and pray to the Christ he saw back in the old country, the man of living gold, will make himself visible to these two young men and spare their lives so they can spend the rest of it earning the greatest glory a man can get, to be humble servant of His Divine Ministry and spread his Gospel.

In a couple weeks, both Ted and Harvey were back in the MRI tube with Alex hardly holding his breath, waiting to see how many light dots will show on the screen.

Then the strangest thing happened. Out of the twenty-eight dots previously in Ted's scan, there were only four, and all above the chin. Harvey had six and all above the chin.

Dr. Baynes were perplexed: "I don't know what you guys have been doing, but whatever it is, carry on. You are on the right track."

Ted was released in four days and put on reduced chemotherapy. Harvey had to stay longer since his cancer was much more advanced.

A couple years had passed since, with Ted completely cured. The brothers assumed that Harvey had also survived even though the lady across the hall had passed away.

Alex was on his way to enter the familiar Country Market to buy some greens when a tall black man blocked his way in. Without even looking up, he just went to the left and was blocked again.

"I will punch this SOB right now," Alex thought angrily and then froze in amazement when looked at the man. The man was Harvey, and right next to him, smiling, was his Mama.

He had changed. His face showed the damages from the cancer, but he was cured and alive, thank you Lord.

"You, you a hard man to get rid of, ain't he Mama? Ted is also doing fine."

Harvey had given up the computer business, been to school to become a Minister and recently accepted a job down in Alabama in a large African American congregation.

"You were telling us that if we survived the curse of cancer, we ought to spend the rest of our lives serving the Ministry of the Lord, and I am about to do just that. Thank you brother for praying and caring for us two terminal men."

"Lord hears our prayer, ain't that right Mama?"

"Amen brother, and thank you," she whispered in tears after giving him a hug.

"Thank you for praying for my baby."

Fifteen years had passed after this inspirational encounter when Alex walked in the familiar Goodwill store on Main Street. Something immediately caught his attention: It was a large, gold embossed Bible, almost new and selling for a dollar. The family never had a Bible since the escape from the old country, where the 300 year old family Bible that had spent nearly a century in the church Father Ivan had built in the Black Rock Mountains was thrown on the street by the furious KGB in the pouring rain, their rage beyond belief having discovered that the family had slipped away from their claws.

So Alex had a Bible, a gift left from a beautiful American human being who had passed away, to replenish the one destroyed by the Evil Communist.

The first corollary of the Reagan Revolution was that the importation of American jobs overseas started a new normal in business whereby a service previously done in one of the States, was now sent to some God forsaken country, with phone centers staffed with people whose English skills and accents were unheard of by most Americans. The carnage was still continuing with more and more companies in Ohio and elsewhere going bankrupt, unable to compete with the dirt cheap foreign labor and resources. Alex started thinking that the "Third Hand" as Benny Ben had suggested, was about to destroy Ohio, the nation's industrial heart, leaving scores of cities in ruins and consequently causing an even bigger crash that will eventually destroy the whole country. Mr. Reagan was playing the role of the American President beautifully, probably being the greatest actor to ever occupy the Oval Office, and despite all predictions of an imminent improvement, the economy was deteriorating still further. Alex met through a mutual friend a young Utah composer, whose sensitive artistic nature has been impressed by the upheaval and the hardship many of his countrymen were going through, so he composed a short opera called "Foreclosure in Vermont" as his graduation work.

The parts were:

1. Overture of the falling Vermont leaves
2. Aria of the Bank officer.
3. Dance of the loan adjusters.
4. Choir of the Court Bailiffs.
5. Duet of the City Judges
6. Dance of the Homeless Flakes

The music for the opera was not recorded at the time and we cannot say if this was a new "Le nozze di Figaro" that will leave a mark on the magnificent edifice of American culture, but it was clear that people were seeing the damage and suffering Mr. Reagan's economic advisers have caused to millions.

To be fair, despite some rough language on the ground, Mr. Reagan will probably be remembered as one of America's greatest presidents due to his great victory of dismantling the Soviet Block, the destruction of the Berlin wall and consequent advent of the European Union. One of the many dimensions of his legacy has not been recognized or explored, however. It is true that Reaganomics caused widespread dislocations with the method of giving tax credits and then writing them down to the national debt, a practice that were to sow the seeds of an even bigger crash than anyone could have ever imagined.

Paradoxically, sending a lot of American business overseas and subsequent laws prohibiting dumping of hazardous chemicals may have made

Mr. Reagan the greatest environmentalist of all time, setting the national cancer rate on a long downtrend, thus saving millions American lives, an honor never recognized or given credit for.

Another and probably the most unpleasant dimension of his legacy is the fact that he left an innumerable number of Ronald Reagan impersonators, tall, with that familiar haircut and conservative suits, enormous shoes, obnoxious, combative and still an eyesore in many Universities, town halls and TV shows. None of them, however, had the elegance, wit and warmth of the Old Master. After all, the man was a natural charmer and communicator.

As President Reagan's term was coming to an end and his Vice President Mr. Bush was about to win the elections, Alex felt the need for an intensive study of possible places within the US where the potential brunt of the coming crushing Depression might be as minimal as possible, guided by his Academic adviser suggestion to look for places with a higher than normal money velocity.

Father Emo, who had of course read the Arabic edition of the Holy Book of the Muslims called Mashary Sharif (the Koran, as it is known in the West), was watching with a great uneasiness the dispatch of American forces to the Saudi Kingdom, which was almost certainly inviting a reprisal by the Wahaby sect, the instigators of what is now called Extreme Islam. So when Iraq's ruler Saddam Hussein invaded Kuwait and President Bush sent troops to Saudi Arabia, the stage was set for a monumental confrontation between the Middle East and America in addition to the already raging first Gulf war.

The administration of President Bush provided the economic stability that was lacking during the roller coaster days of the past eight years, though the real estate values were still subdued after the gold price had collapsed from nearly $860 to $360, even with the war raging in the Middle East.

The family was blessed with another child, Melanie, a little girl very different from her troublemaker brothers, gentle, always ready to smile and give a hug.

Sending the youngsters to school soon made it plain that time had to be spent on every homework, assignment and teacher's concern, just like Alex and Agnes were young again.

So he began working on plan E2E4, a move to West or Southwest in anticipation of the coming crash.

The best candidates were found to be Las Vegas and Miami, with Miami soon rejected because of an absolutely atrocious crime wave of murders and mayhem due to influx of Central America drug dealers, coupled with a complete lack of intervention by the Federal Government in its willingness to start deporting those involved. After all, the Cubans and the Colombians were staunch supporters of the Republican Party, an important voting bloc that could not be lost due to a small matter as few spectacular drug related crimes.

The precise Anglo-Saxon brains of the Republicans' burning desire to balance the cash register on one hand and pay little or no taxes on other were causing deflationary bubbles to pop, having the dubious distinction to have three of the biggest market crashes so far on their watch, that is

1929, 1974 and 1987, with the latest two crashes 13 years apart, usually during a second Presidential term. So assuming Democratic win in the cards after one term of Mr. Bush's presidency in 1992, odds of significant crash sometimes in around year 2005-2009, possibly of the magnitude of 1929 had to be seriously considered.

The economic post-Vietnam war reality seem to be a secular mimic with roots in the annals of American comedy, specifically the famed episode of the Three Stooges called "A plumbing we will go," as one administration will try to fix the economy and then the next will make it worst, with the code words as "bailouts," "injecting liquidity," and "haircuts" commonly used.

The modern actors were:
1. Moe as the Republican.
2. Shemp as the Democrat.
3. Curly as the Independent.
4. The Judiciary as the Cop.
5. The Americans as the house owner.

Some people have argued that the Republicans have been the party of exclusion and limited upward mobility, which is of course not true at all. Since the most spectacular crashes have been mostly on their watch, they have unwittingly presented once in a lifetime opportunities for those disciplined and risk averse American human beings willing and able to buy a valued asset for say 33 cents, and after some time sell it for a dollar, thus finally presenting themselves with a gift of those fine leather shoes the Republicans are so famous for.

The only trick in this proposition is to make yourself lay-off resistant, since all work separations were just a few months before the important lows, and according to the McGregor Theorem, you may have no choice but to buy a set of tires instead of 100 shares of GE right at the geometric bottom of the market.

On other hand, the Democrats would spend years and generous billions to fix the busted lives of those that have been hurt or thrown overboard during the previous cycle, to educate and give a chance to less advantaged, an activity usually accompanied by raise in inflation, taxes and market interventions deeply resented by their counterparts.

So the cycles were rolling over and over, and even though the people on the streets had very clear vision of where America should be heading, exactly as Benny Ben had observed, there seem to be a "Third Hand", a group of Democrats and Republicans legislating laws of a country without borders, debilitated and exported Industrial base, an increasingly uneducated populous carried by the treacherous waves of the popular culture, spreading drug epidemic, and reduced National sovereignty.

In this kind of environment, Alex had to hold a contrarian position on how the children should be educated despite the enormous peer pressure to concentrate on sports instead of reading books, a decision which proved to be almost prophetic in a time horizon of some twenty years.

A new and charming president, the former Governor of the Great State of Arkansas Mr. Bill Clinton arrived on the American scene in 1992, ready to give the country a fresh start, building on the weak recovery that had started under President Bush. He was fortunate to have hired one Robert

Rubin, an experienced Wall Street hand as his
Treasury Secretary, a decision that brought the
Nation employment, real estate and financial
markets back to par after twelve long years of
supply side experiments. One of his first trades was
to execute a large bonds swap in the billions,
setting the stage for economic recovery and
increased employment that carried the DJI over the
magic 10,000 mark for the first time.

    Alex decided to list his property for sale and
head down to the Southwest. He wanted to test the
hypothesis that Las Vegas with its mighty casinos
and large part of income due to international
accounts will be able to endure the severe stress
brought by the continuing exportation of industry
and piling up of deficits by the "Third Hand."

Chapter 7

Plan E2-E4: Escape to the Southwest

On a cloudy March day, Alex and the two boys left Ohio aboard the blue Ford van on what turned to be a seven day trip through the heart of the country from Saint Luis to Joplin Missouri, all the way down to vast plains of Texas and then west to the coast.

Judging by the music, the mystical soul of melting pot America had to be Memphis Tennessee, with the inner country spreading from the Gulf Coast all the way to the Canadian border with fingers of "Children of the Founders" settlements along both the east and west coasts. The Mid-Americans were friendly and ready to help guys, first in St. Luis, fixing a nasty radiator leak, then down in Oklahoma City where the blue Ford got a new distributor cap. But trouble started in the wide open space of West Texas as a late snow storm and howling winds were tossing the van like a match box, Alex following closely a big rig, itself trying to stay in line on the windswept road under dark clouds just above the wind shield. Finally, the rig pulled over in a truck stop and so did Alex, everyone tired, hungry and almost falling asleep.

But this was the Great State of Texas, and happily the lunch special was "One pound burger, mountain of fries and double coke" for about ten dollars, the biggest lunch they had ever seen.

"You better eat well guys, and fill up the truck up to the rim with gas because the next stop is 250 miles away," the attendant advised, a word well intended since back on the road the storm worsened with visibility at most 500 yards, and they were alone in a flat, snow-covered field with vicious gusts of wind literally lifting the van off the ground.

After many hours of drubbing and tossing, eyes red and bleary of trying to see through the falling snow, finally the lights of Amarillo became visible on the horizon.

"We are very happy to make it to your haven, madam," Alex admitted to the motel attendant.

"I say you are the lucky ones," she smiled.

"There are a bunch of cars scattered over the road and the highway patrol is trying to help them before the dark and cold sets in."

The next day, well rested and full with expectations, back on the road they were, with better weather making the faraway blue mountains of New Mexico clearly visible, embracing an endless brush and cactus covered desert punctuated by the occasional clusters of sequoia trees. Everything went well through Arizona until another vicious snowstorm hit right when the blue van started climbing up the mountain near Flagstaff, a storm so sudden and intense that the snow seemed to be growing by the minute. There was no way they could stop and put the tire chains on, since the road boundaries were hardly visible in the white out.

Completely disoriented and confused, no one noticed an hour had passed by, and with the mountain peak behind, suddenly as if in a miracle, the snow stopped and a boundless green alpine forest on both sides reminisced Austria, the road stretching to the horizon.

"Daddy, I think someone is testing us," Allan suggested.

"No wonders the original Americans were such a tough guys."

Going down to the desert along winding roads with occasional crosses on the side, lower hills and less vegetation led finally to Nevada route 95, a road stretching as far as the eye can see, surrounded by lush desert brush and distant sun-scorched mountains that seem to converge to an invisible peak in a maze of puffy white clouds ahead.

The blue Ford was fighting the heat and raising elevation well, and as soon as they had passed the small mining town of Searchlight and reached Railroad pass, a few miles down the mountain gorge began to widen its embrace and there it was in the distance, the jewel of the desert southwest, Las Vegas, spread in a green valley surrounded by tall blue mountains under a bright, indigo sky.

Exhausted and hungry, they stopped for a bite in a small casino on Boulder Highway, met by the blinking lights and sounds of the slot machines as the locals were checking if Lady Luck was around to bless them with a win.

A friend had reserved an apartment for the family in West Las Vegas, warning them not to cross the major street nearby because, "the colors lived in there," and there was a lot of racial tension after recent rioting, protesting segregation and employment discrimination.

It was surprising to hear that major stars like Sammy Davis and others had to look for lodging during a concert tour only in the segregated part of town so many years after the Civil Rights Act had passed and the casinos, still dominated by the mafia, were white only domains.

After a week in the apartment, it was clear that bunch of low lives were residing there, and the family rented a house with the option to buy up west close to the Toyabe National Forest boundary, right at the edge of the desert, where a struggling home building company had built a few models, eager to sell them one.

But there was a problem. The Nevadans were viciously independent people, not very trusting of newcomers and requiring all important papers be on file and checked over before one can get a job or be extended a line of credit. So Alex had to wait for months, supporting the family by trading the market until Agnes could come over and get a job, while the children had joined local schools and tried to find new friends in this distant and unfamiliar place.

But despite what some pundits have called the "Sin City," the local leaders seemed very pragmatic and eager to commit the resources needed to make their universities and schools the best they could be, helped by generous casino donors building new libraries and research laboratories all over.

After a year, Alex was finally able to get a job in the University as Agnes had landed position in the largest hospital in town.

One interesting thing about Nevada was that they evaluated everything and everybody regularly, a practice borrowed from the casinos requirement for a spotless service, something Commandant Glazer could not have survived for more than three months with his habit of being rude and uncompromising, may he rest in peace in the Republican part of Heaven as Cornelius Brown would have said.

Las Vegas had half of its residents speaking Spanish, and so many illegal aliens that the official language in most restaurants was naturally Spanish. In fact, some local people would add an "O" at the end of a name of an establishment to make it more Latino sounding.

During the last few years of President Clinton's term, a steady stream of outsiders were moving to town, attracted by the building boom, generous labor market, still very low prices and naturally the pagan delights of "Sin City" many of us have heard about.

In all fairness, no one in Las Vegas would ever pander gambling, sex, or any other activity to anyone, local or otherwise, as the casinos simply provided the best food, entertainment, lodging, and the rest was up to you. The city had very professional Police Department whose officers were not afraid to shoot when shot at, after this was the Wild West as order was maintained meticulously and every crime investigated until resolved.

So in this atmosphere of stability and order, Alex was very surprised to discover a group of indigenous people named "Azlatan" having weekly meetings in the University's library. They were discussing strategies on how to secede the four corners states from the US, return it back to Mexico, and then put all gringos into the elevator and press the infinity button, if you get the drift.

The leader of the conspirators, a tall skinny man with a goatee and a ponytail, did not hide his hostility toward Alex or in fact, any American person.

"Professor Invador, get your stuff and go back where you came from. It is time for you gringos to leave the land of the Red Man."

"But I did not invade anyone," Alex countered.

" I am just trying to educate you so you can leave the Reservation and find a good paying job and better future for your kids."

It soon became clear that logical arguments did not bode well with the group as some had displayed flashes of violent anger and most would carry at least two small blades, even though having a weapon in the University was a sure way to get one in deep trouble with the police.

The Latino immigrants had large, closely knit families with the majority of the children born in the USA being very polite and hard workers, facing enormous hurdles and poverty. They had to excel in school and college, sincerely hoping that their illegal status will be eventually forgiven and the families would be given a chance to get the dreamed green card, not realizing that the whole immigration question was a cynical tug of war between the political parties, war with no end in sight at all.

A poster child of this invisible war was of course the disabled student Manuel Salsido, an illegal alien so famous that when the immigration police were trained how to apprehend someone, they had his picture on the wall as his friends would joke some time.

Brought in Nevada at the age of one by his mother, Manuel suffered a stroke during his bout with illness that left him with a paralyzed left hand and numb leg. Undeterred by his disability, he graduated from high school and earned a degree in International Finance from the University. Like most illegals, he had purchased Social Security numbers for himself and his sister on the street, and fortunately the numbers were stolen from real American persons and not made up. This distinction provided a safe harbor in the long run until the Federales were eventually able to create a database to cross check for phony Social Security numbers. Manuel landed a dream job in a hamburger joint and was immediately discriminated by his own supervisor, an illegal alien himself, who would assign work hours to friends for a fee and give him only one day a week which is about $50, not enough at all to share the expenses with the sister.

Twenty-six-year-old Manuel was in tears.

"I am about to have another heart attack and die soon. I cannot live in Las Vegas on $50 per week."

Alex suggested that a visit with his district manager would definitely be a plus.

"You are being discriminated on basis of disability by a ruthless person who is selling company's time for money. The management will be surely delighted to hear this."

Delighted they were as the supervisor was fired next day for not smiling at the customers, and Manuel was given five days per week plus overtime.

"What are you doing with all this money Manuel, what?" Alex would joke.

"It is time to open a Forex account so you can get part of the action with those evil Capitalists, you know what I mean? You are going up Homs, just pray the police doesn't get on your tail by chance."

But the victory was short lived as dear Mom Guadalupe was found to have a liver cancer, and the hospital would not provide the costly medicine to an illegal person.

Agnes had heard of a secret fund to help indigenous or homeless people in need of care, and soon Guadalupe was given the medical treatment that prolonged her life for more than a year.

One cold day, just before the end of the fall semester, Manuel came to the office and some of the students noticed that he wore very old, dry sandals without socks, clearly had frozen feet and was shivering.

"Professor Chaikin, we need to find something better for this man to wear in this weather, don't you think?"

Alex remembered that a wealthy Republican colleague of Agnes had given her a pair of marvelous $250 a pair sneakers to gift someone in need, and soon Manuel was the one in them, looking like a member of prestigious golf club on the prowl.

So who said those Republicans are not nice people?

"Gosh Manuel, you'll never get stopped by the police with those sneakers, never," the students would joke.

"In fact, you may also find a rich older woman to go with the brand new look."

The political landscape continued to unravel under the current administration.

First Lady Hillary Clinton was the creator of the famous phrase, "It takes a village to raise a child," something that rang a familiar bell about the march toward the Planetary Government Mr. Reagan and his successors have initiated. Even though President Clinton negotiated with the Republicans to produce a budget surplus and improve employment, the exportation of American jobs and industry continued relentlessly, suggesting the "Third Hand" was firmly in control, with the destruction of the American middle class being the ultimate goal.

Alex was beginning to imagine what the name and background of the first Secretary of the Planetary Commission would be. He clearly had to be an inclusive person, certainly not American, and more to the left than right of the spectrum: Comrade Ibrahim Hon Shu Danielovich Brewster came in mind, a Chinese-born Muslim raised by his Jewish aunt and then adopted by the lesbian couple of Danielovich Brewster.

His first act would have certainly been to fit all cows, horses and seniors citizens with fart suppressors and school curriculum be reduced to shopping, hanging out and smoking pot. Anyone caught studying Algebra was to get 20 lashes in the rear.

The American politicians vision of the "Global Village" was of course re-incarnation of John Lennon song "Imagine," and many being brilliant attorneys, conveniently ignored a small and insignificant detail called Islam, with a billion people guided by the Sharia law, where a major constituency of the Democratic Party, our friends from the Gay Lesbian Freedom Liberation Front will be stoned to death since the bone headed clerics did not buy any of the stuff the progressives were pushing as "our way of life."

But this was nothing new since the same people were dancing in the streets after the fall of the Berlin wall, forgetting that some 20 millions died in the Gulags and wholeheartedly embraced the New Chinese reality, again ignoring the fact

130

that Mao probably killed more people than Stalin.

Some American Politicians had the habit of throwing the bodies overboard, wash the deck and start the party over, guided by the old motto "The market knows best," a proposition that was about to be found null and void some years later.

As the term of President Clinton was drawing to a close despite an impeachment by the Republicans, the booming economy encouraged some gifted casino visionaries to begin building a slew of new European style casinos, which in turn attracted thousands to Vegas and whole new parts of town spread in the desert.

So as President Bush took office, Vegas was on the way up as Paris and any of those nocturnal places on the Riviera you always wanted to visit reincarnated in the Nevada desert, including the European chefs, doormen and naturally most beautiful dancers and entertainers the world has ever seen.

But bad is always following the good, and the drug flow spread not only on the strip but also among the locals.

Alex was hearing from the children that groups of youths would go deep in the desert to party and smoke pot, away from the iron grip of Metro Police, not realizing that soon they became targets of even more potent drugs from which there was no escape.

The drug dealer's route was through the mountains, away from main roads guarded by the police, in a rendezvous with the Mexican cartel mules half way, where they can buy a pound of pot for $800 and then sell it for $5,000 on the streets of Vegas with the hard drugs even more profitable.

The ease with which one could make

money in Vegas was certainly the reason many would not even consider education in their future, even a high school GED.

Why should one spend precious time learning organic chemistry or math when making $50,000 parking cars was the norm and then at night, you can get all the pot, drinks, and lap dances you want. For those of us with flair for mischief, a visit to a swinger club could extinguish even the most passionate fire one can imagine.

"My most cherished dream is to become Assistant Manager of Pacific Motors and then marry my cocktail waiter girlfriend Maggie," a student confided.

"But why not a manager? You'll certainly make more money and get better benefits."

"I don't want to work that hard. Besides, I make more money parking cars than some teachers."

But in life, appearance and substance rarely converge into a happy marriage, and this was certainly true for Southern Nevada.

Despite the label "Sin City" the elitist TV pundits have slapped on Las Vegas, Alex started noticing that below the surface of the easy, entertainment-based lifestyle being its trademark, there was a multitude of crosscurrents that painted a picture of very tense, extremely high technology city operating on the boundaries of known technology in fields reserved for the most famous universities of the country.

The local casinos were prime example of latest high tech applications brought to life so much so that students from countries like Switzerland (world's oldest hoteliers and bankers) would come to learn about the new trends in hospitality management at UNLV.

But there was more. Nevada educational system ratings have been near the bottom of the National list for a long, long time, basically suggesting this was a place of spoon heads, prostitutes and chain smoking gamblers. But when Alex started going around town on garage and estate sales looking for treasures including rare books and manuscripts, he started noticing that someone was reading books and articles on 900 level boundary problems in applied science (800 being the PHD level), and since he had met most of the scientists in the University, it was clear that there was another invisible cultural level, well camouflaged and with purpose not apparently clear at first glance.

There were teams of scientists working with banks of super computers on projects so classified that a friend of his would ask him never to mention his name to anyone during the quarterly meeting of a certain professional association downtown and even refused to sign the visitor roster. The Las Vegas area had one of the highest concentrations of current or retired soldiers from the most elite units of the American Armed Forces working on classified assignments, and Alex observed that there were companies involved in high tech ciphers coding programs and laser applications where only people with advanced degrees and top security clearance could proliferate at all. But the biggest surprise came at 5:45:02 AM one early spring morning when he had stepped outside to pick up his newspaper, just to see a brilliant object in the sky lit by the rays of the rising sun, approaching from north at very high speed in a sky with a few scattered clouds at approximately

18,000 feet. It crossed the 28-mile wide valley in 17 seconds on a southeast course, almost invisible and without any sound when passing just below the clouds, vanishing behind the distant mountains on the horizon, indicating an air speed of some 5,900 miles per hour. So here was an aircraft, crossing one of the most heavily defended air spaces in the world, just miles from Nellis Air Force Base, in plain sight, almost transparent, noiseless, and clearly with advanced propulsion, not being shot down or forced to land.

The hidden charms and pagan delights of Las Vegas were irresistible to a lot of people from around the world, led by so-called new Russian and Chinese entrepreneurs, formerly Communist officials that have plundered whole state enterprises with the blessing of the "New KGB." On location now in Las Vegas, in full view of the world, spending their money like there was no tomorrow while their poor countrymen were struggling in a miserable life of only a few dollars per day.

It was a disgusting charade, lauded by some Americans as a new era in world history, reminiscent to the Dutch Shultz gang dancing on the streets after hearing that Al Capone had been elected a mayor of the city of Chicago.

It was not clear if someone in the government was observing those developments, but Las Vegas was a place to meet the most challenging and front-page individuals one could possibly imagine.

As V.I. Lenin had reportedly said, "The Capitalists would even sell us the rope with which we will hang them."

Chapter 8

A long, worrisome summer

Shadows of scattered signs were appearing in the life of the family, the meaning of which it took some time to understand.

Allan had already graduated from NYU and was working as a civilian employee for the US Coast Guard in the base on Staten Island, so in mid August 2001, Alex got a call from him requesting a loan of $850 to help move from a dormitory next to the North Tower up west toward Central Park in a small one room apartment.

"He does not live here no more, he moved out," was the joking reply as he did not feel sending money to anybody.

Agnes was furious.

"Don't be an idiot. Send the boy the money right away and let him move out soon," she screamed in rage.

The money was reluctantly transferred and proved to be the best investment they ever made. A few days after the confrontation, Alex left Agnes and Melanie in the mall and then went back to the university to pick his assignments for the fall semester.

It was a sunny, breezy day in Vegas with few cars on the road when a red light surprised him, and the car slammed to a stop half way on the crosswalk. There was nobody behind, but Alex noticed two young men leaving the bookstore across the street, and then slowly started crossing right in front of him. One was tall with a blue shirt and jeans, curious slanted eyes, and a bright smile.

The other was short and stocky with a long mustache and burning, reddish eyes, brown flannel shirt and blue pants, obviously a dumb foreigner as the joke goes.

The man with the red eyes did not like Alex's car in the middle of the cross walk, and he literally scraped his pants on the plastic bumper, giving him a look of hatred he hadn't seen since his trouble with the KGB.

Being in a very good mood, Alex was not about to start a fight. He thought the men were Mexicans, but then he had never seen such hatred in the eyes of a Latino person.

The two men lazily entered the UNLV parking lot and vanished in the crowd around the bookstore as he continued to follow them with his eyes in puzzlement and interest until someone in the back honked and told him to get moving.

Alex woke up at 5:25 AM on September 11th, 2001. As if by premonition, he turned the TV on CNN, which was most unusual for him because the first thing he would watch in the morning was the ticker on CNBC Market Channel. Around 5:48 AM, there was a news flash showing a plane hitting the North Tower, raising his blood pressure sky high since he knew Allan had a job interview at 9:00 AM EDT with some record company just across the street. Repeated attempts to get hold of him failed, and then the only thing to do was to call his girlfriend Michele.

"Father Alex," she screamed in the phone.

"A plane just hit the North Tower and Allan wants to go upstairs to help his buddies from the Coast Guard get down to the street, but the police is herding everyone away toward the park. My God, another plane hit the towers, Allan get out, get out..." and then there was a stretch of silence as the phone went dead.

Alex had seen evil before, evil by the way and ease with which human life is taken, and seeing Manhattan Island in clouds of fire and smoke extending to the sky, he knew that America's homeland was a target of the Third Reincarnation of the Prince of Darkness as has been prophesied for a long time, an evil man born somewhere in the Middle East.

The first lecture started at 8:00 AM and he kept talking as in trance with most of the class shocked by the attack and a couple of girls from New York softly sobbing in the back, the material discussed being the last thing on anyone's mind. Alex kept talking, writing formulas and examples on the board without any idea what he was talking about, and finally at 9:20 AM the lecture was over. With the most of the class gone, he noticed two girls dancing and snapping their fingers in the air, reminding him of a Turkish dance he had seen many years ago.

One of the girls was a student of his and the other apparently a visitor.

"We are celebrating the great victory of Holy Sheik Osama bin Laden and Islamic Nation over the Infidels. I am sure my people back in Indonesia are dancing in the streets, I know it."

It took Alex a few minutes to comprehend the indescribable rudeness of this statement, even though he had known many Muslims who held deep resentment toward America and the West due to their support for Israel.

Eyes full with tears with the view of burning towers fresh in his mind, there was no need to start another war now; he simply asked them to leave his classroom, leave immediately.

Back to the Internet, the clouds of smoke billowing over Manhattan brought renewed fear in his heart as he was praying that Allan and Michelle would call soon, even though seeing people running from the towers covered with soot and some visibly injured depressed him further.

Finally, the feared call came on Friday night and thanks Lord, the two and some of their school mates had barricaded themselves in the apartment, unable to open the windows due to the smoke and smell of burning bodies, exhausted and hungry. In a completely brilliant move, the Federal bureaucrats had closed the bridges to the island and cut the supply of food and necessities to thousands trapped inside the war zone, placing checkpoints along all roads that made things even worse.

After visiting the hospital for having a severe nose bleed and breathing difficulties, all have converged to the relative safety of the new apartment and luckily across the street, the sandwich shop as if in a miracle had a dozen subs left, but no bread at all, only cold cuts and condiments.

Allan's only course of action was to call the commanding officer of the Coast Guard Base and ask for help. Help they did, sending a vehicle to pick him up through all check points and then back to Staten Island where he finally got some medical help and hot food.

The base was on full military alert with three circles of defense perimeters, troops on constant readiness since it was not clear if more attacks were on the way, and naval ships were anchored in the harbor.

The Base Chaplain and Allan conducted services on numerous Navy vessels and other troop concentrations since the majority of soldiers were in shock seeing their beloved city on fire extending to the sky and witnesses of the first enemy attack on the homeland.

If ever there was time to test the faith of an American human being, this had to be the one.

Alex had his own shocker to fight with. The men he'd seen crossing the street next to UNLV bookstore appear to bear striking resemblance to two of the hijackers, Hani Hanjur and Navah Al Hasmi, with hundreds of Las Vegans reporting sightings all over town about the same period of time. The loan of $850 which Alex being a cheap skate planned to refuse, had turned out to be the best investment they ever made since many buildings around ground zero have been razed to the ground, surrounded by surreal maze of twisted steel and burning debris where the proud towers once stood.

For Alex and the family, the attack on the American homeland was an incredibly painful thing to watch due to long historical strife with the brutality of the Ottoman Turks. In 1802, founding father Ivan had come home to find his wife and beautiful daughters raped and brutally slain by two Muslims. He killed the perpetrators, buried the women and ran for the mountains, a wanted man until his last breath. On Mother Mary's side, the families fought the Turks for almost 400 years in the Balkans before they went down to the valleys as the Muslims left the country in late 1800s.

So the barbarity of Bin Laden in the name of Islam on September 11, 2001, the second day to live in infamy, was no surprise at all since there were centuries of murder, pillaging and rapes against the gentiles, and anyone who would stand against the invaders guided by the cold efficiency of the Sharia Law. The Al Qaeda terrorists seem to mimic the tactics of the 11th century Ishmaelite sect of murderers that have plunged the Middle East into a string of mayhem and fear.

Yet the Muslims enjoyed one of the greatest cultural upheavals in recorded history during the 1st Caliphate, with momentous contributions in mathematics, astronomy, medicine and other fields too numerous to mention, and in fact the Mauritanian Jews carried some of those treasures into Spain, thus giving the birth of the European Renaissance.

Alex was deeply honored to meet the great Soviet aircraft designer Andrei Tupolev during his brief stop at the local model airplane club in the ancient town of Varna on the Black Sea during the early 60s.

Tupolev was a very kind man and a bit of a gentle philosopher.

"Building and flying an airplane is one of the highest forms of humanity possible. Taking a group of people over restless oceans, snow capped mountains, heat torched desserts and windswept planes, then delivering them to their loved ones on the other side of the world in the best traditions of peace and universal brotherhood of man."

Perhaps the Muslims were to be well advised to use their substantial mental, scientific and material resources in the spirit of the 1st Caliphate to build and fly their own airplanes, instead of playing with explosives and committing war crimes by crashing passenger jets into towers full with security brokers.

But the controversy surrounding the current attack was not to die any time soon. President Bush started to bombing the Taliban sanctuaries in Afghanistan shortly after the attack, a decision that brought warm smiles and sighs of relief on the faces of a lot of Americans, including Alex's. A picture of the President and Mrs. Bush was quickly framed and on the wall of his office with some students exclaiming, "That's a boy, George, give them hell," to the chagrin and dismay of some Middle Eastern types.

Entering one of his classes and glancing over his usual American students, Alex was surprised to see a young man sitting right in front of him having an aura of long, red flames emanating around his ears indicating a violent anger bordering on imminent assault.

"What is your name Sir?" He could not resist the temptation to find out where the student was from since during the thirty years in America, he had seen only one person, a foreigner, with such a concentration of hatred around him.

The man was named Selim, an engineering student from one of the small sheikdoms at the mouth of the Persian Gulf, a son of a wealthy government official who had arrived in Nevada just two weeks ago expecting immediate reprisals and rough treatment from the local Americans, hence the hostile aural signature.

He later brought his friend Ali to the office hour to have a talk, and expressed his amazement for being treated fairly and without any sense of immediate revenge or resentment from anybody.

Ali, a devout Muslim, was very remorseful regarding the attack.

"We have spilled the blood of your people

on our hands, and Allah will punish us for that. May He have mercy on those departed, and we pray that the Americans will forgive us for this terrible crime."

Selim was not remorseful at all.

"I think you should blame your government for the crime. This was a Zionist set-up against Islam to start with, the first step toward destruction of the holy sites of Mecca and Medina."

Here were the fires of war again as the Islamist were blaming President Bush and his Administration for burning down part of a country's largest city, a claim so absurd that made the KGB look like altar boys on Christmas Day, a claim raising Alex's blood pressure to 193 over 167.

"You mean to tell me that Wayne the post office man and bunch of G workers stole the planes and bombed their own city? Let me give you a piece of free advice about these people. If you make three Americans mad, you are in trouble. Osama and his mule heads made 300 million Americans mad as hell, so you better have a place to hide because there will be Special Forces after your asses until there is United States of America. And another thing, I am offended by what you just said. You may come to my office hour, but you are not welcome at all, and you can complain to the University if you like."

Two weeks later, Ali showed up alone, kind of depressed and embarrassed.

"Immigration found out that Selim had entered the US at McCarran airport without an entry visa stamp, and he is to be deported by Friday. It is a pity since his father had supported and sheltered many Americans in our country. You think he can say something in his own defense? He has an American girlfriend and will be absolutely devastated without her."

The news made Alex so sad that a faint smile appeared on his face.

"Well, we finally have a government starting to pay attention, don't we? I wonder who the dimwit woman is? I would be surprised if I have not met her before," a thought went through his mind.

"Well, what you think?" Ali pressed.

"Your friend is offending the American people in a time of great loss and sorrow, even though his father may be a good man who is sheltering the troops from a hostile attack. I think a three-page letter of apology is in order, expressing regret for entering the US without proper documents, extending deepest sympathies for the loss of life and denouncing the Islamo-Fashist slander of the United States Government," Alex advised.

If there is such a thing as an elegant marriage of transcendentality and practicality, it had to be codified in the female gender since everything about women is today, their haircut, makeup, shoes and look, no vision of tomorrow or yesterday, just the wisdom of today, great sensitivity toward the green part of the spectrum with the men just horses pulling the cart forward.

This became abundantly clear when Selim & Co were back in the office hour with his darling girlfriend Sarah Cryson, a student of Alex in his physics class a few semesters ago, whose bar exploits and senseless love relationships were whispered among many and examples for the few bright ones.

Now in love with Selim and a person with substantial experience regarding personal affairs, she could already see the cracks on the walls of her relationship with the devout Muslim who wouldn't share her passion for alcohol and pagan delights, putting himself in a position of authority as required by the Sharia law.

On top of that, the three-page letter to Immigration had been politely accepted and his deportation cancelled with the understanding that at end of the semester he would leave and not be back for five years.

"I can see your beautiful blue Irish eyes sparkling behind the burka and a name tag "wife #537" adorned with diamonds in the harem of your love Selim." Alex joked.

"The only thing I wonder is where in the world would you find a bar to get drunk in the Middle East, a charming place of the dirtiest male chauvinists in the world?"

Sarah was in tears.

"Professor Chaikin, I just don't understand why I must lose the man I love, why me?"

Alex had a theory. The best way to a happy life is the early recognition of losers, brown eye losers, blue eyed losers, lying losers, charming losers, with a loser being a human being who constantly gets mixed up in unfavorable games.

If a person can manage to stay away from losers, then the only logical alternative is to break even or win.

"I understand now, all three men I have fallen in love were losers. But how do I know who is a loser?"

Alex had to introduce her to the twelve rules of finding a mate using the number seven.

After reading the rules, Sarah was amazed by the sudden influx of wisdom coming her way.

"I got beat up and shoved around by these clowns, and it was all so simple Professor, so simple. I have my new target in sight already, and I'll be in touch."

During the second term of President G.W. Bush, and with his personal blessing of course, an aggressive campaign to get a path to citizenship for immigrants like Manuel Salcido was initiated in Congress, even though the public opinion was decidedly against giving people that have broken numerous US laws any breaks at all.

So hundreds of thousands took to the streets in major cities across the nation in a flood of red, Mexican, Salvadorian, and any conceivable flag except the Old Glory, had portraits and tee shirts prominently displaying smiling Che Guevara, led and encouraged by organizations like La Raza and Azlatan.

But being certified law breakers, waving foreign flags, carrying pictures of Communist Revolutionaries, and on top of that demanding citizenship was not brightest thing to do, so the effort melted down and with it the dream of our friend Manuel Salcido to get the beautiful green card.

President Bush seem to have a warm affinity with Mexican drug dealers since he pardoned many and refused for a long time to free agents Ramos and Compean, the two Border Patrol officers who shot the rear of a drug dealer with a few hundred pounds of pot on him and made a mistake in reporting the accident.

So when the sheriff starts jailing his own officers for trying to nail down a reputed drug dealer, people became very confused and frustrated, feelings those were certainly factors in the Republicans' loss of the election, since it was clear that the American sovereignty was ignored and offended for the sake of the hoodlums across the border.

Alex started getting a call every night around 11 PM, a call from a drunken Spanish speaking man.

"Man, this is Ramon. You stole my Celia, Homs, you betrayed me. I trusted you like a brother, Homs and you took my woman."

Manuel, an illegal alien himself, had inserted the following phone message in Alex's phone:

"Esta La Polizia Federal Nice. (This is Federal Police Nice.)

Por Favor: Introduzca uno a ser detenido, (Please enter one to be arrested.)

Dos para ser deportado (two to be deported)."

The annoying calls stopped immediately, yet from time to time they will be back and let some fine Mexican music play, which he did not mind at all.

About that time, Allan was accepted in the Harvard Business School, and Simon had gotten residency in a Boston Hospital associated with the same University, news so improbable for a man who once worked for 39 cents an hour on the docks of Goodwill Industries that he ignored it. It was too much for him, simply too much.

All of a sudden, that magic Northern place where the Pilgrims had set foot on American soil on a rainy day in 1620 on their journey of destiny became a part of family's inner world. Like if by an act of the Providence, Simon's apartment was located a few streets from the Longfellow's house, a house where Founding Father and our first President General George Washington had once lived.

So Alex was counting the days until he would step on the holy soil of Boston, ready to breathe the cold Atlantic air and sense the spirits of those remarkable people about whom he had read so much with nearly religious admiration, walk the streets in their footsteps and pray in the churches where they had found peace and solace in times of fateful junction.

A friend of his, a retired Air Force pilot, had taught him the basics of flying using the MS Flight Simulator. Alex would approach the Logan airport flying low over the ocean just to be surprised how unpredictable the weather over the North Atlantic could be, with a successful touchdown always welcome and hands wet in sweat trying to guide the aircraft through gusts of rain and patches of fog over the harbor.

The actual flight turned out to be even more challenging sitting two rows behind the right wing with full view of the control surfaces, just to see the aircraft bounce in a persistent drizzle and high winds as it started its descent to Boston, circling around for some ten minutes until finally touching down under the masterful hand of the pilot.

"A good landing, thank you very much. Much better than if I were in your place."

The crystal clear spring air and recurring waves of rain were something he had not seen for some time, curiously looking at the old, red brick Tudor houses reminding him of Ohio in the winter, lush grass and vegetation under gray, gloomy sky.

Simon's apartment was in an old brick building with a steam heat, an entrance lined up with a row of brass mail boxes and walls tiles adorned by small swastikas, giving a feeling of someone being transported to the beginning of the 20th Century, feeling amplified by the rusted window rails under overgrown, green leaf trees.

The next day, a taxicab brought the family to the Harvard Square in a silent drizzle, a forgotten memory of a man living on the edge of the Nevada desert, where few inches of rain per year are events remembered for a long time.

A walk through the University and then over the bridge over Charles River brought Alex to the entrance of the Harvard Business School, a complex of red brick buildings with interior yards where the statues of famous alumni adorned manicured gardens with water fountains and Latin inscriptions of great wisdoms.

The Bloomberg Hall had an area where the great business leader expressed his admiration to his father by creating a visual history of his long trek to success. On the basement floor, there was an antique NYSE trading post, complete with brass counters and ticker displays, a place where a long time student of the stock market can stay in awe and think of how much of the world history must have gone through it for the last one hundred years.

This was a place of silent efficiency, spectacular success reaching the sun and people that have changed history, yet Alex, a man who once was paid 39 cents an hour felt awkward and uncomfortable being in the Temple where some of the world greatest entrepreneurs had left their mark. But perhaps that was the miracle of America, where the son of someone who had repaired old furniture with Benny Ben in the bowels of Goodwill Industries, can now join Wall Street and become something impossible to imagine forty years ago.

As people have said, "America, only in America." Back to Harvard Square, Alex was going in the little alleys lined with street vendors, trying to find an old book or souvenir that will capture in time the memory of this proud and elevated place.

A few days later, on the way back from a long walk to the hospital where Simon had his residency, the rain finally ceased as Alex and Agnes found themselves in front of the Longfellow's house, now a national monument since General George Washington had lived there for a while during the Revolutionary War of 1775.

The main building was closed for the season, but grounds were open. After passing by an enormous tree on the side of the house, they entered a garden where Alex was instantly overcome by emotion so brilliant and feeling of beauty and peace so elevated, that started walking around from one flower cluster to another as if he was being led by someone who had waited an eternity to hold his hand and show him this paradise. He was feeling the presence of a spirit, perhaps the aural shadow of General Washington or the wife of Longfellow who had perished in a fire in the main house. It was a spirit of such elevation and shades of gold as seeing Christ again, a spirit that transcended the boundaries of space and time long after the material body had turned into dust blown by the cold northern wind, a voice as a murmur in the whispers of the falling rain.

The Founders had left us the Constitution and Bill of Rights, which many modern Americans were using to take any conceivable point of view and mischief behavior, including rejection of the Christian religion and even saying a prayer in public events.

Enlightened by the spiritual contact with the departed and still feeling the smell of the flowers in his nostrils, Alex thought that ignoring the incredible moral strength and faith of the original Americans was a fatal mistake. The important papers they left us were the most significant writings in recorded history after the Holy Books, a magic trek for peace and guidance in times of trouble, a forgotten and often ignored dimension of the Nation founding.

On the way back west some thirty-thousand feet above the homeland, Alex was thinking about the innumerable powerful civilizations that have perished in the dust ball of time due to one or more errors in their mission statement, praying the fellow citizens would have the eyes to see and hearts to feel the aura of the Founders and return to the great spiritual traditions that had made this country great.

But history has its own heartbeat and voice, and this was becoming very obvious back in Las Vegas as a new American storm was brewing under the surface.

President Bush, a graduate of the Harvard Business School and a compassionate Conservative like his great father, had passed a set of tax cuts that set the economy humming even after the shock of 911 and raging wars.

Life was never better, the steaks and beer flowing like a river and real estate exploding overnight, people unable to comprehend how such a wonderful and happy time may come to an abrupt end.

Year 2007 was a time of great wealth and fortune in Las Vegas as properties had tripled and quadrupled, making people believe that the Nation was on the way to an endless prosperity as many would take home loans and indulge in expensive vacations, cars and other luxuries. Being a college professor who had been studying the Kondratieff wave and other market cycles for years, Alex did not believe any of the above, trying to impress upon his students and anyone that would care to listen that there is only one politically incorrect thing in America. It is called the stock market, and prudence and increased financial education was worth its weight in gold.

But naturally, no one would listen as the party was going on and on.

Alex and Agnes were invited to a Christmas party by a friend of theirs Leah Aldridge, a physician assistant who had just purchased a $480,000 dream home on the Western slopes of the Las Vegas Valley, a home appointed with the best things one can dream of, including a brand new pink Hummer shining on the driveway.

A crowd of faithful admirers gathered, including her former husband, former boyfriend, a Forex trader, current boyfriend and dance partner named the "Big Blue Eyes," and many others too numerous to mention. The most tender filet mignon steaks, exclusive wines and other culinary delights prepared by a top Las Vegas chef adorned the table. Leah had recently won a coveted dancing competition, and the emotional pinnacle of the night was a dance medley where she and her partner dazzled the crowd with a sensual meringue dance, making the evening clearly one of her greatest triumphs.

But there was something very wrong in Las Vegas and across the nation at the time, with many banks aggressively pushing complicated loans exceeding the financial competency and borrowing capacity of the clients, clearly setting the stage for a crash of incredible proportions. The old motto "The market knows all" would suffice no more, and since there was no Federal oversight of the loans, millions of Americans were trapped without any respite at all.

The market started trending down in the summer of 2007 and so did the home prices as more and more people started missing loan payments, leading to mass defaults and bankruptcies. Our friend Leah had signed, (naturally without reading it), an index house loan whereby the home payment would rise from $1200 a month to a whopping $4800 a month, clearly a trap of gigantic proportions. Gone were the pink Hummer and all the wonderful stuff, as she had merengued herself all the way to bankruptcy court, left with the clothes on her back and an old Ford Focus with a busted passenger door.

The Forex trader boyfriend was also bankrupt, unable to protect his market position during the crash, and so was the "Big Blue Eyes" whose employer had laid off everybody due to severe cash shortage.

Being a street smart person and still holding a job, Leah rented a house from her new rich boyfriend, and like a loving mother who would never leave her children in trouble, provided a room to each of her former loves. Everybody was under the same roof again, though naturally not in a dancing mood.

This was the beginning of a new class of white collar homeless people, including a friend of Alex's who would retire to his University rooftop sanctuary to share the night with the pigeons after teaching Calculus and Statistics classes, with the campus police naturally looking the other way since he was a Nam vet and so was the police chief.

Meanwhile Allan and his hedge fund traders friends from the Harvard Business School decided one beautiful Saturday to drive to Marta's vineyard in a brand new blue Bentley for a wine and food tasting party given by a senior Wall Street insider, eager to unload large portfolio of stocks using all the contacts he could muster.

The friends were still profitably trading in the Pacific Basin at night in the hope that upon graduation they could land a coveted job in some of New York's biggest houses. One of them had landed a job in Lehman Brothers with a starting bonus of $75,000 and salary of $180,000 plus benefits, as the market was still fluctuating above current levels without any hint of downside breakout.

But as it has been mentioned previously, the truth is like a septic tank, and the smell will eventually get out no matter how hard we tighten down the hatch.

One charming morning, Allan heard that there is something wrong with Lehman Brothers and naturally phoned his friend Jessop, but then the practical transcendentality of the very bright and far seeing wife intervened by saying, "We need to keep this nest egg ($75,000) for our children's future."

The call was ignored and the next day Lehman Brothers opened at $2 7/8, down from $52 the previous day, and ended up closing at $0.76.

Gone were the bonuses, salary, and benefits including the blue Bentley, and the future had gotten a slap in the mouth as the ensuing crash forced mutual and hedge funds to cut down and fire anyone who had lost money on the trade.

Jessop then found a job as a sale representative for a major fishery along the coast, a position lasting only few months since the supervisor did not appreciate his lack of enthusiasm about the fish business which was understandable, considering the nauseating smell of dead fish one could feel even in his sleep.

The next job offer was a dream, a trader for a major sovereign fund in a Persian Gulf Kingdom starting a year later, an impossibility for an Iraq veteran with a wife, two children and no extra income except his VA benefits and very few dollars in the bank.

So those of us out there who feel that being a Wall Streeter is a breeze should think twice, because it is a dog eat dog arena without any mercy or logic at all.

In the last months of President Bush's term, frantic steps taken by the Federal Reserve to halt the banking crisis did little to stem the slide as major houses like Merrill Lynch and Lehman had failed, and DJI was losing 150 points a day with some 45 days away from zero at current rate, a meltdown of unimaginable proportions.

But the housing crisis was just beginning as more and more people were in default with the number of homeless in Las Vegas and elsewhere up with no end in sight.

The newly minted homeless would be very creative in finding place to shelter, such as shopping centers, where one can beg in the parking lot, get inside, buy something every few hours to avoid trouble with the management, wash up and then be back outside to beg again.

The managers of these outfits were very understanding, and even though one can walk through the store and see a whole family of four with dirty clothes and clearly filthy, the basic American decency would prevail, and people will help at any occasion, including Alex who started carrying a pouch of quarters, ready to throw few when needed.

Melanie has been working at the United Way for some time before her acceptance in the Stanford Law School. Every week, her group would have a homeless project somewhere in Las Vegas with food, clothes and toiletries distributed to people whose sudden descent to the streets had been unthinkable just few years back as many were Ivy League graduates with comfortable positions in society.

A new President Barack Obama was clearly elected in response to the frustrations many Americans felt about the market and housing crash still under way, promising that his Administration will provide "a change you can believe in." The pledge resonated with many as "The market knows best" motto of the Republicans that was naturally blamed for what some pundits called the "Great Recession."

But reality was much more complex than it appeared at first glance.

This storm has been gaining strength stealthily under the surface, as factors and cross currents that have been in play for many years finally lined up their vectors in the same direction,

155

producing a tidal wave of galactic proportions.

If many Americans spent little time educating themselves about contracts and finances, their lives and destinies would have been shielded from the unpredictable swells of the economics of charlatanism, a system where printing money creates mirages in only the up direction, with anyone unprepared to be devoured on the way down.

According to Father Emo, since there were no interest rates in ancient Rome, the lender would tie the right hand of the borrower to his left hand with a piece of dry animal ligament called the "obligazio," a Latin word where the English term "obligation" comes from, holding a whip in the other hand, ready to punish any disobedience.

In medieval Europe the nobility were not particularly bright, and in case whereby a loan was not repaid in time, the honor of the person was offended and suicide was not out of the question.

According to an unconfirmed legend, the practical brain of a Jewish fellow named Count Shlomo Von Wasserstein found a plausible solution: give the lender few gold pieces at the end of the month, then keep the principal amount and live happily thereafter without resorting to extreme measures at all.

The pragmatic logic of the simple interest rates was not enough for the emerging capitalist states. The western economies have found in the compound interest rate model the reincarnation of the Medieval Alchemist dream of creating a "motto perpetuo," a monetary system that can provide an unlimited supply of money to counteract the natural business cycles.

The pinnacle of this kind of thinking was

triumphed in England to be specific, whereby Lord Maynard Keynes's economics of growth and money creation was spreading like a lightning across the Western world, carving the face of the market system as we know it. The meddling with the money supply has been blamed for all economics upheavals and wars that have already claimed in excess of fifty million lives.

So to return to our story, modern Americans who were unfortunate to have many loans and credit cards were wrapped in a web of "obligazios" like cocoons, having surrendered their freedoms and at the complete mercy of the lenders. The lender whip was of course conveniently hidden in the credit card disclosure's small print, enumerating all the horrible consequences of a credit default, a truth that became evident as more and more people were falling behind or completely stopped payments of their loans.

But that was not all. The economic brains behind the "Third Hand" had an even brighter idea: Send as many jobs as possible overseas thus removing wages as major influence on the inflation index, then give generous business tax cuts for outsourcing factories abroad. Open the borders and let anyone who can walk come over, slap any deficits to the national debt account, then print all the money in the world without any noticeable inflation at all. Brilliant, ain't it?

It took thirty years for the smell to get out, but people started noticing that the above proposition had one lingering contradiction. The goods brought to America at great profit for American businesses were to be sold to consumers whose income was trending lower and lower and jobs becoming scarcer by the year. As with all

Ponzi schemes, the cards would eventually fall. Not all civilizations embraced the miracle of the interest rates, however.

The Orthodox Jews were forbidden to charge interest to a fellow Jew. So were the Muslims. The Sharia law forbids charging interest to a fellow Muslim, instead extending "a brotherly loan," where one does not pay interest and can keep the principle amount, a contradiction that set the ever expanding margin accounts of the Western world in a dialectic confrontation with entrenched rules of the Middle East.

As millions of Americans found themselves trapped in a web of "obligazio" cocoons, the endless exportation of American jobs finally undermined the ability of many to support the lifestyle they felt entitled to. The mirage of the "American Dream" was cracking despite the efforts of the Obama Administration to thwart the decline and strengthen the bank system.

Alex started noticing that students who used to come to the university in a luxury car would now come on a moped, and some will plainly walk or take the bus. Horror stories of whole extended families from every possible level of society abound, especially African Americans and Hispanics that have lost their houses and cars due to repossession.

E-mail from Elena, a student who had recently got divorced from her husband provided an even more bizarre account of the troubles some got into along the way.

Alex has been hearing rumors that in the northeast of Las Vegas near the State line, there was an encampment of people who worshipped the Prince of Darkness, affectionately called by some

Lord Satan. Elena and her exorcist clan had brought her recently unemployed husband Ubaldo for an evening of dance and purification, a spiritual journey that would help him find a job and return the family to prosperity.

The poor man was bound, gagged, and covered with aromatic leaves while a circle of thirteen naked women with chamomile flowers in their hair danced around the fire under a full moon chanting, "Helter Skelter chicken bones, Magic Lotus come along," a bizarre cry for help that brought chills to Alex when he heard the story.

As the night grew old, the High priestess and her cohorts finally succumbed to the coca leaves cocktail they have drank earlier and now fallen asleep, leaving Ubaldo still bound next to the fire under a pile of leaves.

With great effort not to alert anyone, he managed to untie himself and almost naked, carefully drove out of the camp. Making a right turn put him on an absolutely dark, lonely road converging to a mountain ridge in the distance under Nevada sky covered with clusters of stars so bright that one only needed to stretch a hand above and reach one.

What Ubaldo did not realize at the time that he was driving north on what a lot of UFO buffs have labeled the Extraterrestrial Highway, leading to one of Earth's most mystical places Area 51. There, according to a local joker, a crowd of space aliens have landed after their planet had run out of strawberries and garlic-laced ice cream.

Driving for more than half an hour, Ubaldo finally realized he had his directions wrong, and after a short stop having observed the soft glow of Las Vegas behind the Sheep Mountain Range on the horizon, he finally made a fortunate left turn and was back on I-95 south, full speed home.

But his troubles were not over by any means. In his zeal to put the unfortunate evening behind him, he did not realize that he was speeding and was horrified to see flashing lights behind him. A mostly naked man without any I.D, driving the car of the High priestess who had a long rap sheet, mostly drugs, turned out to be a juicy treat for the police.

When finally identified, a check of his social security number came back as fake and Ubaldo found himself in the hands of the feared ICE police, possibly facing a deportation back to Mexico, never to see his children again.

But then Lady Luck sent him a smile. Our completely incoherent immigration policy had changed again, this week deporting only sex offenders. Since he had a clean sheet, Ubaldo was back to his children after divorcing the wicked wife, a free man on the streets of Las Vegas.

The story made Alex remember the joke of Benny Ben about requiring the American politicians to spend a weekend in jail with the rest of us, just a slap in the mouth for them to pay attention and stop lying to their constituents.

Was it possible to deport a politician, even for a short period of time, just to give a new frame of reference to a person who is tempted by a mischief?

If one can rectify events by dancing naked around a fire, a lot of the percenter economists and politicians whose policies were the reason for the crash should have been brought to an exorcist dance to put fear in them. Yet no one was brought to justice, as they were upper class, immune from the trials that had besieged the rest of society.

While the market appeared to make a major low after massive intervention by the Federal Reserve to the tune of a few trillions of dollars, housing prices continue their decline. The whiff of deflation put unrelenting pressure on homeowners who had borrowed money against the equity of the property, unleashing a new wave of foreclosures, especially in Las Vegas. Never missing an opportunity for a better profit, the drug dealers would apparently rent a property, then start growing marijuana and mixing meth, thus producing and selling drugs right in city, in many cases using shell business as a cover. But Metro Police was not easy to fool. They would fly above the city with infrared cameras that made the very hot drug houses plainly visible, and some twenty properties in Alex's neighborhood were raided by the DEA, with large sums of money and pot confiscated.

American society was undergoing a major restructuring, with increased crime, unemployment and continuous erosion of the middle class in proportions never seen since the Great Depression of 1929.

Yet the exportation of American jobs continued unabated. In fact, the unemployment rate rose to new highs, nationally and in Nevada, clearly indicating the "Third Hand" was firmly in control.

Manuel Salsido observed that the government had deported in one year more people back to Mexico than in the entire eight years of the Bush Presidency. A pity, Alex thought, the Hispanics being the "Praetorian Guard" of Mr. Obama who had voted for him in hope of getting a

161

green card, false expectation amplified by La Raza and other political organizations.

In fact, Manuel was so mad at the President that he would call him "Bushack Obama," an apparent reference to President Bush's workplace raids some years ago.

The drug war reached a fevering pitch across the border as bullet-ridden bodies were found in mass graves. Yet the politicians continued ignoring the bloody violence that had claimed thousands of lives, instead waging endless wars in the Middle East with great loss of blood and treasure.

Alex had to fly back to Boston for Allan's graduation ceremony where the keynote speaker was an alumnus of HBS and one of the most important leaders of Wall Street. Addressing the graduates and a sea of proud families on the green meadow behind Bloomberg Hall, he talked about the new challenges facing the American free enterprise system in the wake of the biggest market crash after the 1929 Great Depression. Listening to the speech, Alex could not help but observe the incredible pragmatism and brutal simplicity of his world. Diverse groups of millions of people were simply market segments whose sole purpose was to provide streams of energy to the bottom line of the company and anyone who was detrimental to that message was laid off or disposed off in some other way.

In other words, the American corporation was designed to provide services in return for energy, a basic money capacitor whose only purpose was to store more and more energy for its owner, an enterprising person who in all probability had taken significant risk in order to achieve his ends.

In stark contrast to that, the Communist System did not allow private business, hence basic services were provided by the state and there was no reason for anybody to care about profits, a simple truth that Father Emo tried to explain to the hippies some thirty years ago.

At the reception that followed, the family met some of the future business leaders of America and was impressed by their positive nature, quick wit and longing to meet the challenges of Wall Street and the world.

Walking back to Harvard Square, Alex had to get a cup of coffee right across the famous Coop bookstore. Suddenly, a crowd of some twenty plus students walked out of the campus and surrounded him in a wall of foreign languages he had not heard in years. Judging from the little red flames he saw around their shoulders, they were from Asia, and in a few he could clearly see what some have called a soul separation, a dark shadow preceding the person. Alex understood some Turkish and could hear words that sounded like the languages of people from Central Asia like Pashtu, Urdu, Turkmen, and some Arabic, yet they started speaking English as the conversation started to heat up.

"The infidels lost sixteen dogs in Iraq today. A great victory for the believers."

Here it was again, the endless war with people celebrating the falling of sixteen brave American souls in the defense of their country, just a mile from the house of General Washington in the heart of Cambridge, Massachusetts.

"No wonder Mohamed Atta started from Boston. These people are privileged to attend the most prestigious University in the country, a University millions of American students cannot even get close to, yet they celebrate America's loss," he thought to himself. Alex stood up, turned around and said, "Have mercy sometimes, would you?"

They were stunned that someone had heard the words, yet there was no sign of remorse, just obnoxious smiles as they spread to the square.

Back on the plane to New York, Alex was trying to shake away the unpleasant memory of the encounter with the hostile students from Central Asia and think about the coming happy days of the wedding of Allan and Lyudmila, that were to take place at the St. Paul Chapel of Columbia University followed by a reception at Harvard Club of New York. Yet he could not close his eyes, remembering what Mr. Cunningham had said years ago: "The Manitou of America will creep in you, rejoice you when she shines above, and offend and sadden you when she is put down."

Finally at peace, he met the rest of the family at the chapel on the Campus of Columbia University on a hot summer day when a person in his sixties is having trouble breathing, less about smiling. But tradition requires that this is the happiest day in the life of the newlyweds, and smiles were mandatory as the ceremony slowly started taking place. Words of exaltation from the pulpit and music played by some of New York's finest musicians including a world famous piano virtuoso brought tears to the eyes and few missed heart beats.

The reception was in the Harvard Club of New York on 44th street, a place of silent magnificence, oak veneers and furniture all around, stealthy servants and guards, signs of eminence amplified by walls covered with pictures of alumni that had helped shape the world and reached the pinnacle of world power.

As the band started playing and a few drinks had been passed around, Alex proposed a toast:

"To the fathers that are not fortunate to be with us during this momentous occasion. To General Washington, Father Emo, Benny Ben, Mr. Ronny Williamson, Mr. Reagan, Mr. John Cunningham and all other wonderful fathers that have lead us selflessly through this endless trek of discovery of the American soul and spirit. To the Fathers."

It has been said the true men are not supposed to cry, but tears started falling and he was choked up. Forty years had flown away like a flock of white birds, so close you could touch them with your fingertips and so far away that your eyes start to water from the glare of the endless sky, from the happy days on the docks of Goodwill Industries to this place of honor and prestige, in a place called America and only in America.

Back in a plane at thirty-two thousand feet on the way back west, Alex was thinking that he should try to enlist in the military again as he had tried to volunteer in Vietnam, just to experience the honor and glory of serving this great country, a country worth fighting for as Father Emo had observed a long time ago.

Back on the ground in Vegas, the reality was quick to bring his attention to the rapidly deteriorating economic situation as mounting foreclosures, unemployment and expanding federal deficit pared efforts by the government to bring the country back to the expansion track.

Simon was fortunate to get a job as a VA doctor in Texas serving veteran communities ranging from WWII to the present, an assignment that made family and friends very proud. After a few months it started to become clear that the wars in Iraq and Afghanistan were not only draining the Federal Treasury during a period of stagflation, but also creating a new file of veterans with insurmountable mental and health problems unseen during previous conflicts.

For the first time in forty years, Alex had trouble understanding the logic of the US Government.

The Americans were fighting eight wars at the same time, the military, drug, porn, education, sovereignty, budget deficit and debt wars. If Rome was to be used as a yard stick, the days of the greatest empire that ever was would be numbered unless the nation could spring out of the stranglehold of the "Third Hand" as Benny Ben had observed many years ago.

There was a splinter group of the Republican Party calling itself the "Tea Party" after the famous revolt against the British in the Boston Harbor, naturally labeled by the TV pundits as "right wing extremists" that started challenging the power of the Establishment and sending new blood to Congress.

At a large and noisy gathering in the small mining town of Searchlight, the home of Nevada's most favored son Democratic Majority Leader Senator Harry Reid, the crowds protested the newly minted Obama Health Care Law, a law portrayed as the end of the free market system and gross encroachment of American Freedoms.

Alex did not understand the specific complaints against the law, but having spent time in the cancer wards as a volunteer he knew well enough that every American needed a basic health care safety net, the only thing that can prevent someone from joining the hundreds of thousands of homeless Americans already on the streets.

Some Ronald Reagan impersonators in Congress had proposed that people have their health care contributions tied to the stock market, a completely irresponsible suggestion, taking in account how many millions lost their houses due to foreclosure, unable to handle even basic financial transactions.

Alex sincerely wanted to see some of those politicians leave their warm seats in Congress paid by lobbyist money and get their behinds in the market, trade every morning in a volatility swings in excess of 20%, no calls from friendly insiders on the Exchange, on their own, risking their own retirement money.

The TV pundits were dishonest again when someone presented evidence on National TV basically suggesting President Obama was an Al Qaeda sympathizer. The silly claim was soundly defeated few months later when the Special Forces found Osama Bin Laden in Pakistan, putting closure to a ten-year-old National tragedy.

The polarity Alex had observed some forty years ago during the trying days of the Vietnam War was still up and ticking as the former highly educated hippies had risen to the top level of American politics and business world, creating power shifts that could be ignored any longer.

Yet the people of the Tea Party could not be ignored either as it was becoming clear that some entrenched Republican types will be voted out and replaced by independents who were about to challenge the massive power of the "Third Hand" and change the direction the country was going in.

The "Left" created the "Pee" party, a threatening anti-sanitation mob with a very cloudy "message" that soon gained notoriety for releasing their bodily fluids on telephone poles, city sidewalks and parked police cruisers. Aside from the pollution, the message was to occupy and destroy the institutions of the capitalistic system. The American Communists were bad students after all, having laid dormant all these years after the Vietnam War, like a deadly cancer waiting to strike the mortal blow, having organized themselves in tow with Radical Islamists, lazy European Radicals and Anti Semites worldwide.

Yet no one mentioned the core existence of the "Third Hand" and the wholesale exportation of American industry abroad as a new super committee was created to make budget cuts and not surprisingly, all-important decisions were kicked down the road after the elections.

So the only way to correct the situation was the stock market that has been gyrating widely, with volatility so high Alex was unable to produce profits from trading stock options, forcing a liquidation of all positions and getting out completely.

The market uncertainty had skewed the premiums so much that two strikes five points apart were having the same premium no matter what.

Not surprisingly soon after, a trading firm went belly up with some billion dollars missing, and all major brokerages were downgraded by the rating agencies.

The decision makers of course had no intention of backing off. Soon new loans were extended to banks in Europe in a push to quell the crisis.

The deficit problem was actually a very simple matter to solve based on the old Appalachian gas station joke.

A man crossing into Wheeling, West Virginia from Ohio stops at a gas station to get $10 worth of gas, a cup of coffee and a doughnut. He tenders a twenty-dollar bill. The attendant with a big smile on his face gives back an eleven-dollar bill, telling him he can keep the change.

So why can't we do the same?

First, give twenty-four hour notice to turn all coins in to get the new currency, 7 dollars per tollar. The new tollar bill would have the prominent inscription, "In God you trust," and below that, "We keep the change," next to the picture of our smiling Secretary of Treasury and a winking eye on the top of the famous pyramid.

There ain't no way the Tea Party crowds, homeless people and other hoarders will be able to drag all those trash cans filled with quarters to the bank, so right there we reduce the deficit by a trillion or so. Next, since we owe some $15 trillion to those Chinese and Arabs, and 15 is not divisible by 7, we have to make it 14, can't we?

There goes another trillion again. And finally, since the government can keep all the change now, the deficit would be gone soon. Then we can spend money on all those wonderful projects again, like building bridges to nowhere or buying super expensive toilet seats.

It would be wonderful, wouldn't it?

Warm relationships across the Middle East will blossom, with those always smiling brave, unshaved faces of the freedom fighters from the Islamic Jihad loaded with hand grenades waving Kalashnikov rifles, an "Arab Spring" that would finally set us on track toward greatness again as our maternal country, the Islamic Kingdom of Great Britain had done already.

The faith of the country was in the hands of the American Electorate.

Alex was watching the developments with great curiosity since this was a test on whether the spirit of the Founders was still alive and Americans' exceptionalism were able to reverse a decline so acute it seemed almost impossible to imagine.

As the trench warfare continued and many Tea Party candidates replaced the traditional Republican types, the gulf between the combatants grew even wider. The Obama Administration wanted to spend more money to perk up the economy and the Republicans demanding the usual tax and spending cuts, a confrontation clearly of a gigantic proportions, yet no one on each side would propose an immediate end of the wars and wide range of Federal layoffs to curtail spending.

As we have mentioned before in our story, the only thing that could bring an amicable solution of a problem like this in an American environment is the stock market, which can open 2000 points down one somber morning as foreign lenders refuse to buy more Treasury debt.

This scenario was not out of the question since the secular bear market that started in 2001 was moving in a declining channel with a lower bound of 5900 sometime in 2013.

Yet after the re-election of President Obama, there was no willingness to compromise on the budget, hence a sequester in the amount of eighty billion of savings per year was instituted and the can kicked down the road again.

In addition, the Federal Reserve started an eighty five billion per month exclusive bond buying program, basically monetizing the debt by printing money, thus forcing everyone into the stock market and avoiding another crash for the time being.

Alex would have never imagined that the prediction of Benny Ben about the existence of the "Third Hand" will become a reality soon, as the "Establishment" GOP crushed the "Tea Party" revolt, then joined the Obama's New World Disorder to create de-facto "Unified Party USA" and suspend US Constitution.

In addition, buoyed by US shale boom the Federal Reserve unleashed an "Internal Financing" program, thus freeing the Government from the scrutiny of the market place.

American political leadership now had the audacity to select winners and losers in currencies, commodities, industries and in fact whole countries, which in turn was about to spark a deluge of wars and regional conflicts, then re-arrange the International banking order.

But the Doomsday clock was on, with the total National debt projected to be forty trillions by 2040 or about $110,000 per US person, and a new set of momentous events clearly on the horizon.

Chapter 9

The Magic Forest

A bright star in this cloudy sky was the news that Melanie was accepted in the Stanford School of Law, so Alex and Agnes had to fly to the city on the bay and help her prepare for this new and exciting time in her life, continuing the proud humanitarian traditions of Father Emo in helping people fight abuse, discrimination and totalitarian violence.

Having never been in Northern California, the grandiosity of San Francisco Bay and the magic of the city brought a feeling of awe and strange surprise to both.

For quite some time Alex had visions of green cruise missiles with Chinese markings coming from the ocean, making a sharp right turn and then flying over what appeared to be West Coast mountains, sneaking in from the North and striking a city on a grey, windswept bay under an umbrella of cold blue skies.

Originally he thought the city is San Diego, but after visiting there, it did not fit his vision.

So there were the flames of distant future events laying their bloody shadows over this great city on the bay, and his only hope was that this was only a false premonition or one of those bad dreams some of us have from time to time.

Once in San Francisco, it was impossible not to visit the aircraft carrier Hornet moored in Alameda air station, a sister ship of the Hornet lost in the battle of Midway as portrayed in the movie with the same name starring our dear friend Mr.

Charleston Heston as Captain Garth.

Alex had never been on a ship of such size, and was very surprised how emotional it was, even though it had only a few proctors guiding the tours around.

There were spirits plainly visible to him, many as waves of gold a few feet above the floor, rushing towards him as they wanted to touch him and say something, then backing off in the corner of the infirmary and waiting for a while just to appear in the next cabin as wanting to show him around. These were not evil spirits, he felt. These were the spirits of young people who had spent time in this place away from their families and loved ones on a journey of harm and danger. Yet they left all their love with the ship that had brought them back to the safe harbors of the motherland.

As Alex stood on the flight deck of the Hornet overlooking San Francisco Bay, he finally understood the meaning of some of Brenda Lee's most touching songs, songs he heard over the homemade radio back in the old country a long, long time ago. This was music of free people, away from home in service of their country, yet longing for the loved ones so much that they have left a constellation of their aural shadows on a ship that became part of them forever.

Alex had a similar but much scarier encounter earlier with spirits in the Malinta tunnel on Corregidor in the Philippines where the American troops had sought refuge from the Japanese onslaught. Walking in the darkness, he felt as if thousands of fingers were touching his arms and chest, seeking help in a danger so acute that fifty years after the bombardment had stopped, a medium could sense their fear and desperation.

The only thing he could do after those spiritual encounters was to light a big candle in the church and pray, pray that all souls whose presence he felt so vividly would find peace and see the living gold of Christ.

A short trip through Berkeley hippies' quarters near the Telegraph Street area brought in a surprise so sudden that it was difficult to understand.

Walking by the many street vendors selling Nam memorabilia and treasures of the hippies' revolution took the family to the doorsteps of a small boutique where colorful books, clothes, and other artifacts of the era were on display. Something caught Alex's attention at once. It was a very familiar Navy shirt with all decorations in place, a shirt he was sure he had seen before. A young man with dark hair and deep blue eyes greeted them inside.

"Is Tim around today?"

"May I ask who is calling on him please?"

"I like to surprise him, if you don't mind."

And there he was, Tim McHill after nearly twenty-five years had passed, silver dust the time had sprinkled over his head, and Megan, with a large peace necklace and peace blouse next to him.

"Yes, I married the enemy didn't I?" he moaned shyly.

"It took me years to understand there were no hippies or soldiers, just Americans in trouble. I found my peace in the loving arms of Megan, ain't that remarkable?"

It finally became clear why he stopped sending post cards back to Ohio.

When pulled over by the LA police, Tim

was found with more than eight ounces of pot on his person and despite his best efforts to convince the judge that this was related to his war injuries, he was sentenced to a year and a half in the slammer and had to stop the drug trade in order to protect the family. Being a stubborn Irishman, he would not admit a mistake, hence the long silence since.

On the way out, he offered one of his witticisms.

"Don't hate people because you may end up marrying them. I could not believe it at the time, but happened to me."

Walking down the street, the words reverberated in Alex's mind.

"Don't hate people because you may end up marrying them."

Before leaving for Las Vegas, Alex and the family visited the National Muir Woods Monument, place of the oldest rain forest on the planet. It was a long stretch of dense, humid valley flanked by redwood trees so tall that it was difficult to see the sky through the overhang of brush and branches creating a living wall of red, green, and yellow leaves, flowers, and tree bark.

Yet there was a tree down, presumably over two thousand years old, its trunk cleanly cut, showing concentric circles telling the magic story of the rain forest. If ever there was a sign of God's Divine design of America that was it.

At tree circle one, it was a simple red twig, just out of the ground, living in peace, hoping one day to grow big and mighty as his forest brothers and reach the sky.

At the same time on the opposite side of our planet, soldiers of a barbaric army in the ancient city of Jerusalem were crucifying a Rabbi named Immanuel, driving iron spikes through his hands and legs to a cross.

Four hundred or so circles later, the tree has grown to a handsome lad, adorned by fresh and beautiful branches full of color and life.

At the same time, on the other side of the planet, a man called Attila came to the gates of Rome and proclaimed, "I am Attila, sword of the Lord." The arrogant and all wise Romans ignored him at first and then sent their legions after him, and an Empire was lost.

Some seven hundred circles later, the tree had grown so tall it could see a patch of blue above surrounded by peaceful brothers in a forest covered by flowers, leaves and beautiful life.

At the same time, on the other side of the planet, a barbarian army of man called Genghis Khan left pyramids of skulls all over the East and a trail of pillage, torture and mayhem. Genghis had a favorite gesture, moving his thumb from left to right, meaning "Take him," and then the condemned man (including his own son) was beheaded or his back broken by the Khan henchmen, the body then thrown to the desert jackals.

Another eight hundred circles later, the red tree finally could see the sky and sway with the magic winds of west, mighty among the mighty, tallest of the tall.

At the same time, on the other side of the planet a man named Adolph Hitler started a war of ferocity and ugliness never seen before or since, with some fifty-million victims lost.

Then our tree fell down and died during a mighty western storm.

At the same time, on the other side of America, for first time ever, a barbarian called Osama burned down part of Manhattan Island and declared, "I am Osama. Convert or perish." The Americans sent their legions after him, but he slipped like a snake in the caves of Afghanistan and escaped justice for almost ten years.

Was this a sign that God's design for America was to unravel? It is possible that the mighty red trees and the native people who lived in peace on the American Continent for millennia's are trying to tell us something?

Like the overlooked fact that in the last two hundred years, America was involved in many wars (including two World Wars), when in the last 50,000 there were none?

Is it possible that some of the millions who came to the American continent brought with them the curse of the rest of the world?

Will the American spirit overcome the Evil of the "Third Hand" and regain power over its own destiny?

Will the Americans say one day, "The Fathers left us a continent, and we lost it due to foolishness?"

Or will the Americans proudly say, "I went, I saw, I conquered," as the great conqueror had said and live by the Divine covenants of the founders forever

The Endless Beginning

.

Made in the USA
Middletown, DE
15 July 2021